圖書在版編目（CIP）數據

十九世紀中國市井風情：三百六十行/黃時鑒，（美）沙
進主編. —上海：上海古籍出版社，2002
ISBN 7-5325-2606-2

Ⅰ.十... Ⅱ.①黃...②沙... Ⅲ.繪畫－作品綜合集－中
國 Ⅳ.J221

中國版本圖書館CIP數據核字(1999)第52506號

十九世紀中國市井風情
——三百六十行

编著：黃時鑒 （美）沙進
出版：上海古籍出版社
　　　　地址：瑞金二路272號

　　策　劃：張曉敏
　　責任編輯：江建忠　秦志華
　　技術編輯：陳文彪

发行：新華書店上海發行所
印刷：上海中華印刷有限公司

開本　889×1194mm　　1/16　　印張20
版次：1999年12月第1版 2002年7月第2次印刷
書號：ISBN 7-5325-2606-2/J·129
定價：145.00元

CUSTOMS AND CONDITIONS OF CHINESE CITY STREETS IN 19TH CENTURY —— 360 PROFESSIONS IN CHINA

Edited by Shijian Huang & William Sargent

Publisher: Shanghai Classics Publishing House
　　　　272 Ruijin Second Road, 200020 Shanghai

Editor in Plan:　　Zhang Xiaomin
Editor in Charge:　Jiang Jianzhong
　　　　　　　　　　Qin Zhihua
Editor in Technology: Chen Wenbiao
Distributor: Shanghai Branch Xinhua Bookstore
Printer: Shanghai Zhonghua Printing Co., LTD.

16 MO 889×1194mm Printing Pages 20
First Edition December 1999
Second Printing July 2002
ISBN 7-5325-2606-2/J·129

致　謝

我們從 1994 年夏天起的學術交往導致了今天這部畫册的出版。

在這部畫册行將問世之際，我們要特別提到皮博迪·埃塞克斯博物館的行政總監丹·門羅先生和上海古籍出版社的社長李國章先生和總編輯趙昌平先生，由于他們的大力支持，雙方達成了合作出版的協議。

在皮博迪·埃塞克斯博物館方面，戴克斯先生負責全部畫作的攝影，其亞洲出口藏品經理沃林先生負責本項目的實施，他們辛勤有效的工作奠定了本畫册出版的基礎。

在策劃和設計方面，上海古籍出版社中國歷史編輯室主任張曉敏先生花費了許多心血，他的一些建議使畫册更顯光彩，更具品位。責任編輯江建忠、秦志華兩位先生和美術設計葉濤先生精細而富有創意的工作保證了出版的品質。

暨南大學中文系鍾山副教授爲大量畫幅選配清人撰寫的竹枝詞，使畫册增添了文化内涵。中山大學周湘博士爲釋讀畫幅標題的廣州方言用字做了不少調查和考證。

謹向以上諸位先生和女士致以誠摯的深深的謝意。

黄時鑒　沙　進
1999 年 9 月 10 日

ACKNOWLEDGEMENTS

This Album is a result of our academic contact since the summer in 1994.

When the Album is about to be published we should like to specially mention Mr.Dan Monroe, executive director of the Peabody Essex Museum, Mr. Guozhang Li and Changping Zhao, director and general editor of the Shanghai Classics Publishing House. Owing to their active support the both sides reached an agreement for its collaborating publication.

In the Peabody Essex Museum Mr. Jeffrey Dykes completed the photographic work of all pictures, Mr. Eric Wolin was responsible for the execution of this project. They settled the foundation for editing and publishing the Album.

In the Shanghai Classics Publishing House, Mr. Xiaomin Zhang spent a great many energy for scheme and design of this project, his some suggestions caused the Album getting more splendid; the fine, careful and creative work of Mr. Jianzhong Jiang, Zhihua Qin and Yetao, assured the quality of the publication.

Associate Prof. Shan Zhong of Jinan University selected many "zhu-zhi (Bamboo's branch)"poems written in the Qing time for increasing the cultural intention. Dr. Xiang Zhou of Zhongshan University done many investigation and identification in order to explained the words of Cantonese dialect which appeared in the Chinese titles of pictures.

To them, we express our earnest and sincere gratitude.

Shijian Huang & William Sargent
September 10, 1999

2

目 録
CONTENTS

致　謝	1	Acknowledgements	2
"行" 畫標題説明	2	Explanation of Titles of Professions Pictures	2
導　言	1	Introduction	13
蒲呱水粉畫一百幅	1	100 Gouaches by Puqua	1
庭呱綫描畫三百六十幅	103	360 Ink Drawings by Tinqua	103

"行"畫標題説明

　　關于本書册所收這460幅畫上漢文標題，據原文整理；個別原缺者，據畫面添補。錯別字和俗字改正出注。若干專用于廣州方言的字保存原樣，出注稍加解説。要一一弄清這些字的含義以及與它相連的詞組的含義，實非易事。原來以爲，到廣州請教一下，即可明明白白。但實際上不是那麽簡單，因爲相隔一個半世紀以後，時過境遷，現在人們已不大知道那些消逝已久的事物。語言本身也在不斷變化，甚至對同一事物的稱呼，過去與現在都會大不相同。經過仔細的調查研究，有的還要對照畫面進行捉摸，才能大體上一一確定下來。但對于個別字、詞的含義，仍不是很有把握。此外，將漢文標題譯成英文，也頗費推敲，由于文化背景不同，個別語詞很難找到恰當的對譯詞，也只好加注稍作解釋，但仍感難盡人意。不當之處，祈請指正。

——編者

Each original picture has a Chinese title; only very few are missed, now added in accordante with their images. All titles are translated into English, and some notes are offered.

——Editors

導　言

"三百六十行，行行出狀元。"這是一句中國流傳已久的諺語。三百六十行乃是對街坊市井各種謀生行當的通稱。隨着中國社會經濟的發展，城市街道上的行當日漸增多。宋元時代已有一百二十行的說法。到了明代中葉（15 世紀末 16 世紀初）已經增爲三百六十行，這個泛稱行當衆多的數字

廣州十三行同文街一景，19 世紀，拉維涅畫
比切博斯刻印，設色石版畫。
New China Street,19th Century,by lauvergne,
Lithographed by Bichebois,Coloured lithograph

一直延用至今。這本畫册就是 19 世紀上半葉中國三百六十行的真實寫照，它所描繪的是當時廣州的市井生活。①

　　儘管"三百六十行"幾乎中國人都能順口説出，可是如果讓誰一一歷數三百六十個行當，這就給人出了一個難題。事實上，不要説沒有這樣的口傳資料，即使是在浩如煙海的漢文文獻中，迄今也還未能發現這樣的載錄。可喜的是，我們在美國馬塞諸塞州賽倫市的皮博迪·埃塞克斯博物館裹發現了一套19 世紀 30 年代的庭呱所繪的中國外銷畫，正好是 360 幅，描繪的又是廣州的市井行當，只有極少數的例外。此外，該博物館還有一套 18 世紀末蒲呱所繪的同一題材的 100 幅中國外銷水粉畫；這些水粉畫不僅色彩繽紛，而且可

賽倫海關（黃時鑒攝）
Customs House in Salem (photographed by
　Shijian Huang)

以彌補那套360幅綫描畫在行當總數上略有不足的缺憾。現在，我們將這460幅圖畫首次匯印成這本畫冊，題爲《十九世紀中國市井風情——三百六十行》，呈現在讀者面前。

在討論這兩套行當畫以前，讓我們先大致回顧一下中國外銷畫。隨着16世紀末歐洲天主教傳教士入華，西洋繪畫也漸漸流入中國。從18世紀初起，馬國賢(Matteo Ripa, 1682-1745)和郎世寧(Giuseppe Castiglione, 1688-1766)等人將西畫技法傳入清廷，而且影響及于一些宮廷畫家、文人畫家以及民間畫家（如姑蘇版畫②）。到了18世紀後期，西法在北京宮廷和文人中的影響日漸式微，但受其明顯影響的廣州中國外銷畫却方興未艾，而且在19世紀初、中期已臻成熟。這是中西藝術交流史上的重要篇章。

從17世紀後期起，中國畫已開始被帶入歐洲。早期的中國畫輸出歐洲，通常都是來華貿易船上的商人和船員的個人販運，一般説來，數量有限。不過，有時候其數量也頗爲可觀，例如英國高斯特林船長在1727年即運送了4箱畫。③當然，這些都是地道的中國畫，不是現在所説的外銷畫。

大約從1720年起，如今被稱作中國外銷畫的藝術品種開始出現在廣州。對于早期的中國外銷畫，人們所知甚少。存世的中國外銷畫，絕大多數都是18世紀70年代以後的作品。所謂中國外銷畫，當具備兩個要素：一、由中國畫師繪製而專供輸出國外市場，通常是銷往歐洲，後也及于美國；二、在繪製時不同程度地采用西洋繪畫的技法，包括透視法、色彩暈染、形式和材料。顯然，這種外銷畫既有別于傳統的中國畫，一般説來又不同于地道的西洋畫，儘管其中有些畫已經洋味十足。

除了"中國外銷畫"這個名稱，它們也被稱作"中國貿易畫"，因爲它們是中國貿易的一部分。在西方，這兩個名稱是被交替使用的。值得注意的是，當時在漢文中已有"洋畫"一詞，這個用詞正好出現在皮博迪·埃塞克斯博物館收藏的庭呱的另一本畫冊的封底題字上面。在此封底題字上庭呱將自己開的店鋪稱爲"洋畫鋪"。

外銷畫有許多品種：油畫（畫在畫布或象牙上）、玻璃畫（又稱鏡畫）、水彩畫和水粉畫（畫在紙、葉或象牙上），等等。就題材而言，則可大致區分爲典儀（如朝觀、巡幸、閱兵）；事件（如談判、剿滅海盜、廣州大火）；海事（如船舶、港口、要塞、商館）；屋景（如十三行、店鋪、庭

庭呱畫册的封面之一，1851年，香港霍斯曼與高德弗萊公司展品。
A Cover of Tingqua's Album, 1851, an exhibit of Horstmann and Godfrey Ltd of Hong Kong.

院、居室）；人物（洋人、行商、官員、官夫人、士兵、婦女、兒童）；生産（稻、茶、瓷、蠶絲、玻璃）；花卉鳥獸；風俗信仰；以及市井行當等等。對這些繁雜題材的需求，反映了當時西方人士對中國方方面面的濃厚興趣。

18世紀時，中國外銷工藝品，包括扇子、墻紙、絲綢和瓷器（"廣彩"或"洋彩"），在歐洲備受青睞。作爲回應，歐洲人的"中國風"應運而生；"中國風"乃是在裝飾藝術方面的中國風格的西方詮釋。洋人對中國的興趣，爲各種中國外銷畫源源不斷地輸出西方開闢了一個興旺的市場。這些中國題材的畫作乃是當時西方人關於中國的景色、文化和習俗的一個主要的信息來源，因而産生了深遠的影響。

從現存的大量作品可以看出，各個畫種所顯現的西洋繪畫影響是頗有區別的。油畫是剛從西方傳入的新的畫種。玻璃畫采用油畫技法，畫在一面，而其反面則供觀賞。兩者均既臨摹西方的作品，又描繪中國的人物和場景。某些題材的作品也往往被反復摹繪，如浩官等人的肖像畫、港

伊利莎白·惠特蘭夫人像，1800-1805 年
中國，史貝霖繪
油彩布本，李查·惠特蘭船長捐贈
Portrait of Elizabeth Wheatland, 1800-1805
China, Spoilum
Oil on canvas, Gift of Richard Wheatland

華盛頓像，約 1800 年
中國佚名畫家
玻璃畫
George Washington, c.1800
China, unknown artist
Reverse painting on glass

澳門南灣景色，約 1830 年
中國佚名畫家
油彩布本，拉塞爾·佩因先生捐贈
View of the Praya Grande, c.1830
China, unknown artist
Oil on canvas, Gift of Mr.R.S.Paine

湯盤，約 1733 年
中國外銷瓷器
芒森·坎貝爾藏品
Soup Plate, c.1733
China, export porcelain
The Munson Campbell Collection

灣景色和珠江口的風景畫，等等。水彩畫和水粉畫，一般說來畫幅較小，似乎更宜于繪製具有中國特色的廣泛題材。

中國外銷畫在采納西洋透視法和色彩暈染的同時，保留着一些中國繪畫傳統；但從 18 世紀末葉起，那些傳統開始發生變化。這裏不可能對此詳加討論，但有一個基本事實需要提一下：不止一幅中國人或西人的畫作顯示，當時廣州的畫師已使用畫版并將它竪起來作畫；但同時，他們繼續使用毛筆，而且還是原來的那種寫作書法和長卷時的執握方法。

水彩畫和水粉畫一般畫在紙上，中國紙和西洋紙都用，也畫在絹、葉和一些工藝品上，如象牙、扇面、鼻烟壺上。進入 19 世紀以後，通草紙（文獻中也誤作"米紙"）常被用于繪畫，英文文獻中也常提及。④通草紙脆薄易碎，但其大小、價格和特殊的紙面結構頗適宜于繪製水彩水粉畫。⑤當時，歐美的紙張已輸入中國，其中一部分也被用于繪製外銷畫。這些歐美紙張上的水印，十分有助于認定外銷水彩水粉畫繪製的大致年代。此外，在 18 世紀 20 年代初，歐洲的洋顏料也已經輸入廣州。⑥

水彩畫和水粉畫占有中國外銷畫市場的最大份額，這部分是由于它們比油畫或玻璃畫較小，繪製所費時間也較少，因而

洋顏料，約 19 世紀中葉
Foreign paints
c.middle 19th century

從河南眺望十三商館，約1852年

庭呱，水粉畫

克拉拉·柯蒂斯女士捐贈

The Hongs of Canton,c.1852

Tingqua,gouache

Gift of Miss Clara Curtis

售價較低。爲了適應市場的需求，畫師所設的畫鋪往往采取各有分工的流水作業方式進行繪製，每一畫匠只畫整個作品的一部分。⑦甚至有這樣的記載：設計好的圖樣的輪廓先用木版輕輕印出。也往往采用隔着透明紙從底本描出圖樣的方法。有時也出售綫描圖，但多半是着色後再行銷售。

水彩畫和水粉畫大多被合訂成册或集裝成盒，也有蝴蝶本以至長卷，但比較少見。許多水彩畫和水粉畫以12幅爲一組（一套）出售，這可能是dozen這個西方計數詞傳入中國的結果，後來中國人稱之爲"一打"。本畫册所收的360幅綫描畫原來即被裝訂成三册，每册120幅，正是10打之數。但是，也有一些是13幅畫組成一套的，不知是何緣故。或許是"賣一打送一張"的生意經所致！

在廣州繪製并出售中國外銷畫的此類畫鋪始于何時，今已難以確考，或可追溯到18世紀中期。這種畫鋪的鋪主本人就是畫師，由他雇傭一些畫工和店員。這些畫鋪都開設在十三行地區的靖遠街和同文街，即洋人所稱的舊中國街和新中國街。衛三畏在1848年寫到，在廣州，畫工多達兩三千人，某些從事繪畫，而某些則在其它裝飾工藝部門工作。⑧奧斯曼德·提凡尼在1849年記載："舊中國街和新中國街的畫工們是一個爲數衆多的階層。"⑨

畫鋪往往以鋪主即畫師的姓名別號命名。今留下名號的畫師僅40人左右，佚名者當不在少數。從現存的作品看，留下名號的人，其多數堪稱畫家無疑。在19世紀20至50年代，最著名的油畫家是關喬昌，別號啉呱。稍後，他的四弟關聯昌，字俊卿⑩，別號庭呱，在1830至1870年活躍于廣州和香港畫苑，擅長水彩水粉畫。可以這樣説，啉呱和庭呱關氏兄弟乃是當時中國外銷畫的主要代表人物中的兩位。

本畫册所收的360幅綫描畫乃是庭呱及其畫鋪的作品。庭呱又作廷呱、聽呱，西文作Tingqua。當時的廣州外銷畫家，都有一個西文拼音的別號，這多半是爲了便于洋人稱呼，好做生意。"呱"字似出自"官"字。那時十三行商人往往捐有頂戴，他們的別號通常末帶"官"字。他們多是福建人，這個"官"字便有了福建方言qua的讀音，洋人稱之也習以爲常。畫師們的別號末帶"呱"(qua)音，當是從行商別號的"官"字借過來的；但他們未捐頂戴，便巧妙地在書寫時以同音的"呱"字取而代之。正因爲只是一個供洋人稱呼的別號，其漢文用字也就不太講究，于是關聯昌的別號會出現庭呱、廷呱和聽呱三種寫法。

前已述及的外銷畫的種種題材，在庭呱畫鋪內幾乎無所不包。紐約大都會博物館存有署名Tingqua的在象牙飾牌上繪製的浩官水彩肖像。著名的庭呱水彩水粉畫册，皮博迪·埃塞克斯博物館原有兩套：一套56幅，一套34幅；香港藝術館所藏一套，原計99幅，今存其主要部分。

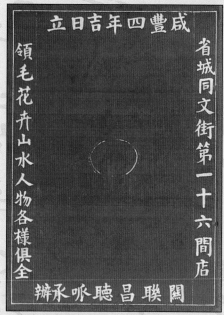

一本庭呱畫册的封底，1854年
Back cover of an album of
Tingqua Studio, 1854

皮博迪·埃塞克斯博物館還有一本聽呱的畫册，外封用玫瑰紅綢子裝幀，封面繪有花飾，封底上下左右寫有白字：上端橫書"咸豐四年吉日立"，下端橫書"關聯昌聽呱承辦"，右邊竪書"省城同文街第一十六間店"，左邊竪書"翎毛花卉山水人物各樣俱全"。此畫册首頁是一幅黑色綫描肖像，很可能是庭呱本人，而後是"各樣俱全"的48幅彩色水粉畫。從其各種畫樣和封底下端文字"聽呱承辦"可以推想，這是供顧客挑選的樣册。從上述封底又可得知，除了現貨交易，顧客也能據此樣册選樣訂購。

1996年，霍斯特曼與高德弗萊公司在香港展出過另一套庭呱畫室的水粉畫，共74幅，包括風景、家室、交易、肖像等等，封面漢字題爲"關廷呱各款什錦"，上款寫"粵東省城第拾伍間關聯昌洋畫鋪"，下款寫"咸豐元年新月吉日立"。這一套"各款什錦"畫册也是在新年伊始設立的，但鑒于它的裝幀十分精美，上述題字筆迹端正，且用金粉寫在黑漆封面上，因而它可能是供出售的什錦畫册。又可注意的是，這裏寫出"關聯昌洋畫鋪"在"第拾伍間"，與上述皮博迪·埃塞克斯博物館畫册上寫的"第一十六間店"相差一號。很難想象庭呱畫鋪中人會寫錯自己的門牌號。可能的解釋是：從咸豐元

6

年至四年(1851—1854)的四年間，這家洋畫鋪或者搬過鋪面，或者它由第十五間擴大到了第十六間。

庭呱畫鋪的室內場景當時也被繪製成一幅外銷畫，此畫現在一般被稱爲"庭呱畫室"。（見附圖）如今存本仍有不少，所畫內容大體相同，稍有差異。此

庭呱畫室，約1855年
水粉畫
Tingqua's Studio,c.1855
Watercolor

畫室內的建築細節、擺設和展示的畫作，既有中西合璧的風格，又仍頗具中國的格調和情趣，尤其是廳中懸挂着的中式對聯和題字。此畫上方正中的題字，可以見到兩種：一種用漢文題爲"靜觀自得"，另一種用英文寫出"TINGQUA"字樣。人們似可從這幅畫的景觀感受到中國藝術家爲西方創作時的某些實際手法。

正是從這間畫鋪，庭呱及其畫工們將各種題材的水彩水粉外銷畫繪製出來，流布到了歐美各地。有人說啉呱作爲一個畫家優于其弟庭呱，但庭呱的繪畫在品質上也有其重要的藝術價值，而且其畫室的作品在産銷的數量上無疑是首屈一指的。就現存于世的庭呱作品而言，其數量也當居第一。僅僅是皮博迪·埃塞克斯博物館的收藏即達640幅。

本畫冊所收的100幅水粉畫是蒲呱的作品。蒲呱是18世紀後期中國外銷畫家中尚知其名的三位畫家之一，其他兩位便是史貝霖(Spoilum)和秦呱(Cinqua)。比諸庭呱，關于蒲呱我們所知很少。當1784年美國的"中國皇后"號初航中國時，蒲呱曾爲莫里斯夫人的衣箱作了玻璃畫。有一張蒲呱爲製作六幅描繪中國皇后和貴族的玻璃畫而開的收據仍被保存下來。1800年梅森(G.H. Mason)在倫敦出版了一本題爲《中國服裝》的畫冊，共收有60幅點雕畫，描繪的是中國街市的各種行當，每幅畫署明"Puqua, Canton, Delin"，表明其原作確實出自蒲呱之手。⑪蒲呱原作很少存世，因而皮博迪·埃塞克斯博物館所藏的這100幅水粉畫是十分珍貴的傳世佳作。從它們的構圖與風格，并比對梅森的印本，可以確認，這些未署名的畫乃是蒲呱的作品無疑。

下面分別對本冊所收的庭呱的360幅綫描畫和蒲呱的100幅水粉畫作一簡

要記述。

庭呱的 360 幅綫描畫，每幅均爲長 30.9 厘米 × 寬 29.8 厘米，繪于 1830—1836 年間。分編爲三册，每册 120 幅。編目爲: AE 21010.A.1—120, B.121—240, C.241—360。另有第四册, D.361—480，是其它題材的 120 幅畫。四册均有紙簽，上印 "TINGQUA" 標記，可據以斷定它們都是庭呱的作品。這四本畫册原屬美國馬塞諸塞州依普斯維奇鎮從事對華貿易的商人奧古斯汀·希爾德，其後裔代代承傳，直至 1931 年爲皮博迪·埃塞克斯博物館購藏。

ABC 三册分別標有漢文福、禄、壽三字。每幅畫上均有漢文標題，僅有個別缺標；約 200 幅又有用鉛筆譯釋的英文，在每册畫作前面還有 19 世紀的英文譯釋的

看傀儡戲，1800 年
蒲呱原作
點雕畫，自梅森《中國服裝》，倫敦，1800 年
Watching Puppet Show
Original painting by Puqua
Stipple engraving, From G.H.Mason's *The Costumes of China*, London, 1800

目錄。漢文標題當是原畫所有，但書寫者文化水平不高，有明顯的錯別字，也有俗字；以及一些標寫廣州方言的特別的字。英文的譯釋也存在不少有悖畫作原意的誤差。在原有記載的基礎上，我們進一步加以考訂，逐一確定漢文標題的書寫和含義，并給出英文譯文，必要時還加

中式庭院，19 世紀中葉
庭呱，水粉畫
Chinese Architcture, middle 19th century
Tingqua, gouache

上簡明注釋。原來缺失標題的，今據畫面予以添補。原畫僅作黑色綫描，標題文字粗糙，裝幀也很簡陋，從這些情況看，它們原來當是庭呱畫鋪供畫工使用

葡萄牙婦女，1854年
庭呱，水粉畫
Portuguese Woman,1854
Tingqua,gouache

的底本。

這360幅畫，我們認爲可以看作"360行"。當然，仔細推敲，也還有些問題。從第1幅到第18幅與製茶有關的畫，恐怕難以一一列爲十八行。又，在這360幅畫中，有重復的，如"賣月餅"(84,224)、"賣新文"(90,252)、"賣關刀"(99,202)、"塗沙佬"(103,127)、"賣咸菜"(115,200)、"綉鞋"(263,352)；有近似的，如"算命先生"(49)與"睇相先生"(81)與"看相先生"(269)、"賣馬蹄"(69)與"水鷄賣馬蹄"(343)、"賣花"（花束，74）與"賣花"（盆花，270）、"化香米"(73)與"化錢米"(145)、"賣木魚書"（行販，148）與"賣木魚書"（擺攤，262）、"賣蘿白蒜"(185)與"賣蘿白葱蒜"(258)、"賣頭篦"(192)與"賣梳篦"(339)；還有個別畫面不能視作行業，如"梳粧"(36)、"疍婦"(58)、"發瘋妹"(346)，等等。如果剔除這些重複、近似以及不是行業的，則360之數仍然缺了一些。這裏也可見出庭呱畫這360行作爲樣本，可能并無一定之規，亦無精心設計，大致上湊足360幅畫就算數了。不過，庭呱畫册雖缺失了一些行當，而在蒲呱的畫册中却又出現了其它一些行當。

皮博迪·埃塞克斯博物館所藏的蒲呱的100幅水粉畫原屬英國的查爾斯·約翰(Charles John, 5th Baron Dimsdale of Meesdon Manor)。100幅畫分成兩册，每册50幅，每幅原大38.1厘米高×28.9厘米寬，上有紅色數字編號和墨色漢文標題，若干幅上還有鉛筆書寫的法文譯文，但字迹不很清楚。這些法文無疑是18世紀的書寫法，參考上述蒲呱18世紀後期繪畫活動的資料，可將這批水粉畫推測爲18世紀末的作品。

蒲呱的這些水粉畫早于庭呱的作品，它們也是描繪行當的畫，而且是這種題材的外銷畫的早期佳作。前已提到，梅森在1800年根據蒲呱的這類畫作在倫敦出版了準確複製的點雕畫册，題爲《中國服裝》。現在這100幅畫數量更大，而且是原作，其品質比梅森出版的複製品自是更勝一籌。

蒲呱這100幅畫的多數標題可見于上述庭呱的綫描畫。但是，也有28幅畫是蒲呱所獨具的，不見于庭呱之作。它們是："澆燭"(10)、"整弓箭"(11)、"做鞭杆"(12)、"山水梅湯"(18)、"弄雀"(20)、"寫畫"(21)、"車夫"(22)、"補瓷缸"(23)、"整架"(26)、"裱扇面"(29)、"鑽珠"(32)、"賣絨綫"(33)、"整番鞋"

（35）、"賣猫"（37）、"踎鼓"（44）、"整夾萬"（45）、"唱獨脚戲"（52）、"舞馬驪"（54）、"描金漆器"（55）、"織布"（57）、"磨面"（58）、"鑿石"（61）、"修養"（63）、"整天平"（68）、"刨烟"（69）、**"按花"**（72）、"打薄餅"（76）和"做箱"（80）。蒲呱這些獨有的畫幅可以彌補庭呱的上述行當畫的不足。

蒲呱與庭呱的這些行當畫足以表明，在18世紀末迄至19世紀中葉的廣州街市上確確實實存在着傳統諺語所説的360行。有了這兩套畫册，我們現在可以認知與看到每一行當的名稱和圖像。

近二十年來，18、19世紀的中國外銷畫越來越受到學術界、博物館以及收藏家、商人和拍賣行的關注。當這些受到西方影響的中國藝術作品逐漸引起重視的時候，人們如今認識到它們有助于瞭解東方與西方交流的歷史和文化的價值。從1970年起在歐美和香港不斷出現討論中國外銷畫的論文和著作。而中國大陸在1987年才開始發表劉海粟的一篇短文《藍閣的鱗爪》（《中國美術報》1987年第5期），相關的研究從此漸漸啟動。最近，胡光華寫成題爲《西方繪畫東漸中國"第二途徑"研究——十八、十九世紀中國貿易畫研究》的博士論文（南京藝術學院，1998年）。這個領域的研究仍在發展之中，我們相信，在中國和西方，都存在着對此課題作進一步考察的廣闊前景。

一部完整的中國美術史應該含有民間美術，包括中國外銷畫。將西方藝術作品導入中國的貿易和由此產生的中外交流也應該包括進來，不要老是專注于對朗世寧之輩的反復討論。現在人們已認識到，從18世紀起西畫的影響已越出中國宮廷，深入民間。姑蘇版年畫已被認爲是具有"仿泰西筆意"。廣州繪製"洋畫"的百年以上的豐厚傳統宜當更多地加以研究，俾使中國和西方不會失缺東西文化交流史上的這一重要篇章。

對于中國學人來説，一大遺憾是，在中國外銷畫的原產地中國大陸，如今却幾乎没有收藏。這類作品的現存收藏散布在曾是其銷售市場的西方世界各地，儘管皮博迪·埃塞克斯博物館具有這類繪畫的世界上最大的收藏，有關的專門出版物却很少，自近二百年前梅森的《中國服裝》刊布以來，本畫册乃是有關中國街市行當的第一部專集。

本畫册是描繪20世紀以前的中國街市行當的外銷畫的首次集中刊印。翻閱這些藝術作品，當年

花卉，約1855年
庭呱，水粉畫
Floral,c.1855
Tingqua,gouache

廣州市井的衆生相即刻呈現在我們眼前，豐富多采，栩栩如生。亨特曾經這樣記載廣州商館的廣場：“中國人常常把廣場當作通衢大道，一些沿街叫賣的小商販也喜歡麇集在這裏做些小本生意。這些小商販有賣鹹橄欖、賣花生、賣糕點、賣茶水、賣粥的，還賣許多其他吃的喝的東西，……後來，又來了一個賣滑稽曲本的。……離他不遠的地方可能看到一個變戲法的，……還有鞋匠在補各種各樣的舊鞋，裁縫整治那些早已失去新鮮光澤的衣服。還有翻修油紙傘的，還有一個編織細藤條的，……”⑫應說這是對當時廣州街頭生活的具體生動的描寫；但是，與這本畫册相比，這段文字描寫就顯得頗爲不足了。

在一幅一幅欣賞優美畫面時，讀者們也會在其它方面有很多發現。如蒲呱所畫的“整番鞋”(35)，這無疑是最早的中國人製作皮鞋的圖像。如蒲呱的“車魚缸”(77)、庭呱的“車玻璃”(21)和“吹玻璃”(25)，表現了在廣州發展起來的玻璃業。又如庭呱的“看西洋景”(56)，可能是這種新玩藝兒最早的圖像記錄。

庭呱的“賣新文”(90、255)和“貼新文紙”(161)，記錄了廣州街頭一種十分值得注意的新的文化現象。從1827年起，英文的Canton Register(《廣州紀事》)在廣州出版；1833年，中國最早漢文報刊《東西洋考每月統記傳》也在廣州創刊。19世紀30年代在廣州街頭賣的和貼的“新文”，大約就是這類新近出現的報刊。順便説一句，新文、新文紙，當是英語news、newspaper的意譯詞，後來也譯作新聞、新聞紙。有如這一事例那樣，我們相信，除了一般地用作中國外銷畫的研究，社會史、經濟史和文化史等領域的專家將會從這本畫册的各種圖象發現新的資料。

中國外銷畫經常表現一些中國歷史與文化的片斷的題材，描繪細膩，富有特色。今天它們的特殊魅力可能比當年初創之時更爲強烈，使人凝目，催人探索。除了它們的藝術水平，人們更多地致力于去認知它們的歷史文化價值。作爲一種特殊的媒介，它們使西方人更好地瞭解中國。

在中國傳統文化的一些精粹開始傳入歐美的同時，更多的西方人實際上是從大量輸入歐美的各種中國工藝品來感知中國的。在這裏，中國外銷畫所起的作用實在不能低估，因爲它們是形象的、引人注目的、題材十分廣泛的。獲得這些畫册和單幅作品的西方人，將它們在歐美各地收藏和展示，廣爲傳播。這些信息是如此廣泛生動，只要看此一册就足以想象這類作品會多麼令人驚嘆。顯然，在攝影術傳入中國以前，中國外銷畫在將中國文化圖像呈現給西方方面起了積極的作用。而且就某些題材而言，如三百六十行，即使是攝影術也未曾留下更爲充分和完整的如此具有歷史意義的記錄。

黃時鑒　沙進

1999年8月

① 歐美人士對這類題材的中國外銷畫給過各種名稱，如商人、商販與工匠、街頭貿易、日常生活、中國習俗，等等。看來當時和現在收藏、經營和研究這類畫的西方人都并不知道中國有"三百六十行"之説。

② 關于姑蘇版畫，可參考[日]青木茂、小林光宏監修：《中國洋風畫展——從明末至清代的繪畫、版畫、插圖本》，圖録（第375—411頁），町田市立國際版畫美術館，1995年；莫小也《乾隆年間姑蘇版所見西畫之影響》，載黃時鑒主編：《東西交流論譚》，上海文藝出版社，1998年，第215—229頁。

③ 參見 Craig Clunas, *Chinese Export Watercolours*, Victoria and Albert Museum, 1984,p.10.

④ 關于"米紙"實際上是以豆科植物通草爲原料製成的紙，在英文文獻中，德庇時在其1836年出版的《中國總述》一書中已有明記。(John Francis Davis, *The Chinese: a General Description of the Empire of China and Its Inhabitants*, New York, 1836,rep. 1972, p.15.)

⑤ 衛三畏在其1848年出版的《中國》(S.W.Williams, *Middle Kingdom*, London, 1848.)一書中曾具體描述這種紙的表面結構如何適宜于接受色彩，可參考該書第2卷第175頁。

⑥ 在1823年出版的馬禮遜所著《中國與廣州港札記》(Robert Morrison, *Notes Concerning China and the Port of Canton,*…Malacca,1823.)一書中收有一篇譯自漢文原稿的"關于抵達廣州的歐洲船隻與貿易"的文獻，内含一份詳細的進出口商品税表，其中有一項即爲"洋顏料"。

⑦ Old Nick, *La Chine Ouverte*, Paris, 1845,p.58.

⑧ 上揭衛三畏《中國》，第2卷第175頁。

⑨ Osmand Tiffany, *The Canton Chinese, or the American's Sojourn in the Celestial Empire*, Boston & Cambridge: James Munroe and Co., 1849,p.83.

⑩ 中匾有漢文題字的"庭呱畫室"圖，在題字"静觀自得"下方的落款中，寫有"俊卿四兄雅屬"諸字，可據以確定庭呱在兄弟中排行第四。

⑪ 梅森曾是英國駐印度馬德拉斯的士兵，在1790年到過廣州，并在那裏買了一套蒲呱的水粉畫。返回英國後，他出版了一本題名爲"中國服裝"的畫册，蒲呱的原畫已由米勒(W. Miller)改作成點雕畫。但顯然保存了原型，并在每幅畫的左下角都雕印出"Puqua, Canton, Delin"字樣。參見 George Henry Mason, *The Costumes of China,* London, 1800; Carl L. Crossman,*The Decorative Arts of the China Trade:Paintings, Furnishings and Exotic Curiosities*, Antique Collectors' Club, Suffolk, England, 1991, p.185.

⑫ William C. Hunter, *Bits of Old China*, London, 1855; rep. Taipei, 1966, p.13.

INTRODUCTION

There is a proverb circulated for a long time in China:"There are 360 professions, each has its own topmost master." The "360 professions" is a general term for all types of professions in Chinese city streets. In the Song and Yuan times (918 — 1368),there had been a similar saying referring to 120 professions. Along with the development and growth of social and economic life in China, the number of professions gradually increased. By the middle period of the Ming Dynasty (from the end of the fifteenth century and the beginning of sixteenth century), the number had risen to 360. This album is a true portrait of those 360 professions in the first half of nineteenth century and show the street life of the city of Canton (Guangzhou) at that time.[1]

Almost every Chinese knows the proverb yet no one can say what the professions are. It seems that there is no relevant record in Chinese traditional documents identifying them. Therefore, it is a pleasure to find at the Peabody Essex Museum, Salem, Massachusetts (USA), a set of ink drawings by Tingqua in the 1830s that depict the 360 professions of the city streets of Canton. In addition, the Museum also possesses a set of one hundred Chinese export gouache paintings of the same subjects at the end of eighteenth century by Puqua; these richly painted and colorful illustrations can supply some depth of understanding of the trades absent in the ink drawings. Now, they are put together and published for the first time in one album entitled:*The Customs and Conditions of Chinese City Streets in 19th*

同文街上一店鋪，1825-1830 年，佚名中國畫家
A shop in the New China Street,
1825-1830,unknown Chinese artist

Century: 360 Professions in China.

Before discussing these two sets of paintings, we should look back at Chinese Export paintings in general. Western drawings and paintings gradually flowed into the Middle Kingdom along with European Catholic priests entered into China since the end of sixteenth century. Since the beginning of eighteenth century Matteo Ripa (1682—1745),Giuseppe Castiglione (1688—1766), and others introduced the techniques of western art in China. Their influence was first attained as painters in the court, then spread to the literati, and finally among

賽倫市的東方中心——美國國家航海史遺址
（黃時鑒攝）
Orientation Center——Salem Maritime National Historic Site
(photographed by Shijian Huang)

the popular artists (for instance, the Suzhou woodcut[2]).The influence of western art declined within the court in the late eighteenth century, even as it was increasing in Canton, reaching its maturity in the nineteenth century. This is an important chapter in the history of art interactions between China and the West.

Chinese painting had been brought to Europe since the late seventeenth century. Paintings were commonly exported in small number as private trade by officers and ships crews engaged in the China trade. Sometimes, however, the numbers were more considerable Captain Francis Gostlin carried four cases of pictures from China to England in 1727.[3] These paintings were thoroughly in the Chinese taste and not those considered now as export paintings.

The category of art now considered as "Chinese export painting" appeared in Canton about 1720. Only a few of those early paintings are known now, the majority of existing export paintings having been made after the 1770s. Two essential factors identify what are called Chinese export paintings:1, they were painted by Chinese painters for export to a foreign market, generally European and then also American ; 2, the methods of western painting, including perspective, chiaroscuro, style, and materials were adopted by the Chinese paint-ers. It is clear that they are not only different from traditional Chinese painting, but also generally distinguishable from paintings of Western origin.

Besides the general term "Chinese export painting"(referring to the fact that they were made for export),such works have also been called "China trade painting"(referring to the fact that they were part of the China trade); both terms are used interchangeably in the West. The term "foreign painting" (洋畫, yang-hua) is found on the back cover of another album by Tingqua. He identified his shop on the cover of this album as "foreign painting shop" (洋畫鋪, yang-hua pu) as well.

Chinese export paintings took many forms: oil on canvas and ivory, reverse painting on glass, watercolor and gouache on paper, leaf and ivory, etc. The various subjects can be classified as: rites (visiting at court, the emperor inspecting, reviewing troops),events (negotia-tions, executing pirates, Canton fire), maritime affairs (ships, ports, fortresses, factories), building spectacles (trading com-pany, shop, house with courtyard, living room), figures (foreigners, factory mer-chants, mandarins and their wives, shoul-ders, women, children), manufactures (rice, tea, porcelain, silk, glass), flora and fauna; customs and beliefs; as well as profes-sions in city streets, and so on. The de-mand for these various kinds of paint-ings reflected the interest in China held by Westerners.

In the eighteenth century, Chi-nese export decorative arts, includ-ing fans, wallpapers, silks and porce-

義盛像,1800~1805年
中國,史貝霖繪
油彩布本,托瑪斯·沃德船長捐贈
Portrait of Eshing,1800~1805
China,Spoilum
Oil on canvas,Gift of Thomas W.Ward

15

廣州商館——烈火蔓延，約 1822 年
中國，畫家佚名
油彩布本，以無名氏基金購藏
The Canton Fire of 1822, c.1822
China, unknown artist
Oil on canvas, Purchased with funds donated anonymously

lain, reached a peak of popularity. In response, Europeans developed chinoiserie, the western interpretation of Chinese styles in decorative arts and interiors. This foreign interest in China created a healthy market for paintings of all sorts to be continuously exported to the West. The paintings of Chinese subjects were a major source of information on the landscapes, culture and custom of that country and would exert a profound and lasting impression in the West.

It can be seen from the great quantity of extant works that various type of paintings each reflected their own specific influences. Oil painting was a new medium introduced from the West. Glass painting was executed in oil but on the reverse of the surface to be seen and painted in reverse order. Scenes derived from Western prints, as well as scenes of Chinese landscapes or people, were often depicted in both media. Many of the subjects were recopied frequently, such as the portrait of Houqua, port views, and the landscapes along Zhujiang (the Pearl River), etc.

Some Chinese painting traditions were preserved when western perspective and chiaroscuro were first employed, but by the end of the eighteenth century, those traditions began to change. One of the essential transformations in technique, recorded in views of artists at work, was that the Chinese artists erected the painting boards when they used it for drawing, but they continued to use a brush in the traditional way, that is, held vertically as is done in calli-graphy and scroll painting.

The watercolor and gouache was generally painted on either West-

從游廊上遠眺南灣,1840 年
中國,畫家佚名
水粉畫,斯蒂芬・惠特蘭先生捐贈
View of the Praya Grande from a Porch,1840s
China,unknown artist
Gouache,Gift of Mr.Stephen Wheatland

ern or Chinese paper, but silk and other surfaces were also used such as leaf, ivory, snuff bottles, and fans. At the beginning of the nineteenth century pith paper(the pith of mulberry tree, erroneously called "rice paper")was frequently used for Chinese export paintings and is frequently mentioned in English language documents; in Chinese it is "tong cao zhi"(通草紙).[4] Pith paper was thin and fragile, but its size, price and special structure were particularly well-suited for the production of inexpensive water-based paintings.[5] At that time western papers had been imported into China,and some of them were employed for export paintings. Watermarks on the papers allow us to identify a date before which the painting could not have been made. Foreign paints(洋顏料,yang yan liao)were known to have been imported into Canton from Europe in the early 1820s.[6]

Watercolor and gouache paintings constituted the largest segment of the market for Chinese export paintings, in part because the production time was shorter and the size was smaller than oil or glass paintings, and so was the cost subsequently. In order to meet the market demand, artists established studios with a production line method where each member of the studio would only draw or paint one part of the whole work.[7] In one surviving example the outline of the desired design has been lightly printed from a wood engraving. It is also common for the design to be traced from an original model through the transparent paper. In some instances the line drawing is sold as well, and in others colors are added.

Most watercolor and gouache paintings were bound as a album or collected in a box, but a few were also mounted as a butterfly book or a long scroll. Many were sold as a set of twelve paintings. The word "dozen" had been introduced into and used in China where it was later referred to as "yi da" (一打). The 360 ink drawings in this album were originally bound as three albums, each with 120 pictures, or 10 dozen pictures. However, some other sets were composed of 13 pictures. What is the reason? Perhaps it was a selling point, the so-called "buy a dozen, get one free!"

It is difficult to know when the concept of a studio started for the production of Chinese export paintings sold in Canton. It may have started in the middle of the eighteenth century. The master of the studio was an artist who employed some artisans and clerks. These studios were generally set up in Jing-yuan street and Tong-wen street(Old China Street and New China Street as they were called by Westerners)in the area of the Western Factories. In 1848 another writer, S. Wells Williams, wrote that there were as many as 2,000 to 3,000 artisans in Canton, some engaged in painting and others in the other production of other decorative arts.[8] Osmand Tiffany recorded in 1849 that, "The painters are a numerous class in old and new China streets." [9]

Usually the studio was named after the master artist's name or nickname. Now only about forty names are known although the number of anonymous artists would far exceed that. Looking at the extant paintings we can say that most studio masters who preserved their names were indeed accomplished artists. During the 1820s—1850s, the most famous oil painter was Lamqua(啉呱),whose formal name was Guan Qiaochang(關喬昌). Shortly after, his forth brother Tingqua(庭呱), whose formal name was Guan Lianchang(關聯昌), secondary formal name Jun-qing (俊卿) [10], also became accomplished in watercolor and gouache, and was an animated member of the painting circles of Canton and Hong Kong in the 1830—1870s. It could be said that Lamqua and Tingqua are two of the main figures in the field of Chinese export paintings.

The 360 ink drawings in this album were by Tingqua and his studio. The name Ting had at least three writing characters in

Chinese: 庭, 廷, and 聽. Chinese artists in Canton working for the export market usually had nicknames with western spelling that were suitable and convenient for use by foreigners. The Chinese factory merchant, or Hang(Hong,in Cantonese) merchant, always had a nickname with a suffix-qua (官, officer), that they acquired by buying an official title. Most of them were from Fujian province, so the pronunciation -qua was also a Fujian dialect. Perhaps the artist's nickname with -qua was a formality borrowed from the merchants, but since they would not have had an official title, they used another character with the same pronunciation.

The different kinds of subjects in export paintings mentioned above can almost all be found in the works of Tingqua's studio. There is a watercolor portrait on ivory of Houqua with Tingqua's signature in the Metropolitan Museum of Art, New York (USA).There are two sets of Tingqua's gouaches in the Peabody Essex Museum, one including fifty-six paintings, one with thirty-four paintings. Another set is in the Hong Kong Museum of Art that originally included ninety-nine pictures, its main part is extant now.

啉呱自畫像，
油彩布本，1840 年代後期。
Lam Qua,self-portrait,
Oil on canvas,Late 1840s

The Peabody Essex Museum also has an album by Tingqua with covers of rose red silk painted with ornamental designs on the front cover, and writing in white Chinese characters on the back cover. The inscriptions read: above, "To set up on an auspicious day, fourth year of the Xianfeng(1854)"; below, "Undertaken by Guan Lianchang, Tingqua"; right, "The sixteenth shop on the Chinese New Street in Province City (Canton)"; left, "There are assorted paintings, bird and animal, flower, mountain and river, figure" .The first page of this album is an ink drawing most probably of Tingqua himself, then forty-eight gouache paintings of various subjects. Considering that this album includes various subjects and the words"Undertaken by Guan Lianchang, Tingqua", it could be assumed that this was a model album from which customers could choose the paintings they wanted to buy. It is also obvious from the cover inscriptions that, aside from on-the-spot purchases, one could order albums or pictures based on the models within the album.

In 1996 the Horstmann and Godfrey Ltd of Hong Kong held an exhibit entitled "Paintings from the Tingqua Studio".This consisted of an album of seventy-four gouache paintings including landscapes, domestic scenes, trades, portraits, etc. These had been bound in an album as well, the cover of which had three lines of Chinese characters. The middle line was "Guan Tingqua, with assorted paintings".On the right, "capital city of Canton province, the fifteenth shop, Guan Lianchang's Foreign Painting Studio". On the left, "To set up on an auspicious day, first year of Xianfeng (1851)." This album was also set up at the beginning of a New Year. However, considering its elegant binding of black lacquer cover with gold powder inscription, and its layout, the album may have been produced for sale. Moreover, it should be noticed that the writing said "Guan Lianchang's Foreign Painting Studio" was at "the fifteenth shop". This is a deviation from "the sixteenth shop" identified on the Peabody Essex Museum's album mentioned above. It is improbable that anyone in Tingqua's studio would inscribe a wrong address. The explanation may be that this studio moved its location, or expanded from "the fifteenth" to "the sixteenth" between 1851 and 1854, from the first year to the fourth year of Xianfeng.

The inside scene of Tingqua's shop was also produced as an export

一本庭呱畫册的封面，約1854年

Front cover of an album of Tingqua studio, c.1854

painting at that time and is known as "Tingqua Studio" (see illustration) . There are several copies of this picture with some variations, but their main contents are the same. The architectural details, the furnishings and pictures visible within the studio reflect a mix of Chinese and Western styles, but the view is most obviously one of a Chinese studio with various Chinese inscriptions visible, including an antithetical couplet. Two kinds of inscriptions in the upper middle in two different copies, one with four characters "Jing Guan Zi De "(Looking calmly, getting by oneself),and another with the name "TINGQUA" in English. It seems that this view of Tingqua's studio suggests some of the practical methods of creating works in China for the West.

From this studio, Tingqua and his artisans created a great many export watercolors and gouaches with assorted subjects that were disseminated through Europe and America. It has been suggested that Lamqua was a better artist than his younger brother Tingqua, but the quality of Tingqua's work is also of great artistic value and certainly the quantity of his studio's output is unmatched.In the Peabody Essex Museum alone there are over 640 paintings attributed to Tingqua's studio.

The one-hundred gouache paintings reproduced in this present album are by Puqua (蒲呱). Puqua is one of three artists working in the late eighteenth century for the export market whose names are still known; the other two are Spoilum and Cinqua. Compared to Tingqua, very little is known about Puqua. When the American ship "Empress

庭呱畫室，約1855年
水粉畫
里奧·霍德若夫伉儷捐贈
Tingqua's Studio,c.1855
Gouache
Gift of Mr.& Mrs. Leo A.
Hodroff

of China" first arrived in China in 1784, Puqua created a reverse painting on glass for Mrs. Morris' trunk. A receipt from Puqua for six glass paintings depicting the empress and nobles of China is still preserved. In 1800, G.H. Mason published an album entitled *The Costumes of China*, with sixty stipple engravings depicting assorted professions on Chinese city streets. Each print contains the legend, "Puqua, Canton, Delin." Indicating that they were indeed taken from originals by this Chinese artist.[11] The extant works of Puqua are few, so these one-hundred gouaches in the Peabody Essex Museum are a very rare compilation. According to their composition and style, compared to the Mason copies, it can be safely assumed that these otherwise unsigned works are by Puqua.

The Tingqua ink drawings and Puqua gouaches

Tingqua's 360 ink drawings, 1830—1836, are each 30.9 cm.H × 29.8 cm.W. They were compiled as three albums, each with 120 individual pictures. The catalog numbers are AE21,010.A.1—120, B. 121—240, C.241—360. There is a fourth album with the number D.361—480 that consists of 120 drawings of other subjects. These four albums each carry the paper

整番鞋，1800 年
蒲呱原作
點雕畫，自梅森《中國服裝》，倫敦，1800 年
Making Foreign Shoes, 1800
Original painting by Puqua
Stipple engraving, from G.H.Mason's *The Costumes of China*, London, 1800

label stamped "TINGQUA", and all four originally belonged to the American China trade merchant Augustine Heard of Ipswich, Massachusetts(USA) and descended in his family until they were acquired by the Peabody Essex Museum in 1931.

The albums A, B and C are respectively inscribed with three Chinese characters: Fu (福, good luck), Lu (禄, high position)and Shou (壽, long life). There are Chinese titles on each picture; only a few of the titles have been lost. About 200 pictures have English translations and explanations written in pencil, and there is a nineteenth century English catalogue of

蒸酒，1800 年
蒲呱原作
點雕畫，自梅森《中國服裝》，倫敦，1800 年
Distilling Liquor,1800
Original painting by Puqua
Stipple engraving,From G.H.Mason's *The Costumes of China*, London,1800

every work at the beginning of each album. The Chinese inscriptions have some inaccuracies and include some informal, popular forms of characters, as well as special characters of expressing the Canton dialect. The English translations also contain misunderstandings of the original intentions of the artist. Based on original records and other existing works, identifications are explained here, with the actual characters and meaning of the Chinese title. The English translations and explanations are defined for each, and necessary descriptions are briefly noted with each relative picture. Where lacking ,titles have been added in accordance with the picture's contents. The paintings were only drawn with black line,the words of titles were not accurate, the binding was simple and crude, so that they should originally be the sample books employed by artisans in the Tingqua Studio.

These pictures could be recognized as "the 360 professions", although some discrepancies need to be identified. The first pictures of tea production, from number 1 to 18, may be difficult to identify as 18 separate professions. Some illustrations are repeated, for instance: "Selling Moon Cake" (84,224), "Selling Newspaper"(90,252), "Selling Guan's Sword"(99,202), "A Man Panning Sand" (103,127), "Selling Salty Vegetable" (115,200), "Embroidering Woman's Shoe"(263,352).Others illustrations may be

中國園林，19 世紀中葉
庭呱，水粉畫
Chinese Garden,middle 19th century
Tingqua,gouache

paired with similar pictures, for instance: "A Master Predicting Fortune" (49)and "A Physiognomist"(81,269), "Selling Water Chestnut"(69)and "A Boat Girl Selling Water Chestnut"(343),"Selling Flower"(bouquet,73) and "Selling Flower"(pot flower,270), "Soliciting for Alms"(73)and "Soliciting Money and Rice"(145), "A Peddler Selling Wooden Fish Book"(148)and "A Stall Keeper Selling Wooden Fish Book"(262),"Selling Radish and Garlic"(185)and "Selling Radish,Scallion and Garlic"(258), "Selling Dense - Toothed Comb"(192)and "Selling Comb"(339).There are several pictures that do not seem to describe professions, for instance:"Hair-Dressing"(36), "Tanka Woman"(58),"Insane Girl"(346),and so on. It appears that Tingqua made the 360 illustrations as samples, possibly without a certain plan and a precise design, they just

中國官員，1854 年
庭呱，水粉畫
Chinese Mandarin,1854
Tingqua,gouache

roughly wanted to get 360 pictures together for expressing 360 professions.While some professions are omitted in the Tingqua album, there are others that emerge in the album of Puqua's paintings.

The Peabody Essex Museum's collection of 100 Puqua gouaches was originally owned by Charles John, 5th Baron Dimsdale of Meesdon Manor, England. The gouaches are divided into two albums of fifty

中國婦女，1854 年
庭呱，水粉畫
Chinese Woman,1854
Tingqua,gouache

paintings each. The original size of each picture is 38.1 cm.H × 28.9 cm.W. There are red Arabic numbers and black Chinese titles on each. Some of the paintings bear French inscriptions of the eighteenth century in pencil, but they are often not very clear. According to these French inscriptions and some contemporary painting materials of Puqua mentioned above, these gouaches could be suggested as the works at the end of the eighteenth century.

These paintings are earlier works than Tingqua's but they too depict professions and they are among the earliest and best of this genre of export painting. G.H.Mason published a book of stipple engravings after some of Puqua's original gouaches, as *The Costumes of China* (London, 1800)which while fairly accurate as reproductions can not compare with the superior quality of Puqua's originals.

Most title of Puqua's paintings can also be seen in the 360 drawings by Tingqua. However, there are twenty eight views represented in Puqua's work that are not seen in Tingqua's. These include "A Candle Maker"(10), "A Bow and Arrow Maker"(11), "A Whip and Rod Maker"(12), "A Plum Juice Vendor"(18), "A Bird Trainer"(20), "A Painter"(21),"A Wheelbarrow Pusher"(22),"A Chinaware Repairman" (23), "A Picture Frame Maker"(26), "Mounting Paper Fan 'Face'"(29), "A Jeweler"(32),"A Knitting Wool Peddler"(33),"Making Foreign Shoes" (35), "A Cat Peddler"(37), "Repairing Drum"(44), "Making Trunk"(45),

"A Monodrama Player"(52), "A Monkey Trainer"(54), "A Lacquerware Painter with Gold Color"(55), "A Lady Weaver"(57), "A Miller Milling Flour"(58), "A Mason Chiseling Stone"(61), "A Traveling Physician Specializing in Hemorrhoids"(63), "A Precision Balance Maker"(68), "Shaving Tobacco Leaves"(69), "Twisting Cotton"(72), "Beating Thin Pan-cake"(76)and "Making Chest"(80).Therefore,these Puqua paintings can supplement the gaps and omissions in Tingqua' s 360 drawings.

These paintings and drawings by Puqua and Tingqua of street professions are sufficient to express that the traditional saying referring to "360 professions" exactly existed on Canton streets at the end of the eighteenth century and into the middle of nineteenth century. We have now, with these two sets of albums, been able to identify and see each name and image of the professions.

In the last twenty years Chinese export paintings of the eighteenth and nineteenth centuries have been more and more noticed by academics and museums, as well as collectors, dealers and auction houses. Their value in helping us to understand the history and culture of East-West interactions is now recognized, as the quality of these Western-inspired works of Chinese art are growing in appreciation. Since the 1970s, some articles and books in the field of Chinese export paintings emerged in Europe and America. From a short paper by Haisu Liu entitled "The Fragments of Lamqua" published in Chinese in 1987(Chinese Art News, 1987, no.5),the field has grown in scope in the PRC until, most recently, Mr. Guanghua Hu's *A Study on the Chinese Trade Paintings in the 18th and 19th Centuries* (PhD thesis, Nanjing Art College, 1998). The study of this field is still developing and we believe there is a wide range of possibilities for future explorations on this subject in both China and the West.

Popular paintings, including China trade paintings, should be contained in a complete history of Chinese fine art. The trade that introduced Western works of art to China and the interactions that occurred should also be included in such courses, beyond the already much discussed works of Giuseppe Castiglione. Most recently the influence of western art since the eighteenth century has been recognized to have extended well beyond the court, deep into the lives of the people in China. Suzhou's Spring Festival pictures are now recognized to have imitated Western styles. The rich tradition of over 100 years of producing "foreign pictures" in Canton, and later in other port cities, should be studied in more depth so that both China and the West will not lose this important page in the history of culture communication between China and the West.

For Chinese scholars, the great regret is that there are now almost no collections of these works on the Chinese continent, their place of origin. The existing collections of Chinese export paintings are scattered throughout the Western world, their intended market, though the Peabody Essex Museum houses perhaps the largest collection in the world of this type of art. There are very few publications dealing exclusively with this subject, and this volume is the first since Mason's book of nearly two hundred years ago to depict the professions so extensively.

This publication is the first ever to concentrate on Chinese export paintings and drawings of the professions found on the city streets of China before the twentieth century. Looking at these works of art, the faces of many people become visible to us, rich and colorful, alive and vital. William C. Hunter described the Factory Square of Canton in 1855:"…the Chinese constantly made use of it as a thoroughfare, and it became the resort of itinerant peddlers and hawkers in a small way of business. There were sellers of pickled olives, ground nuts, pastry, tea, congee(hot rice water), with a host of other eatables and drinkables, …Then again, a dealer in comic songs,… Not far from him might be seen a juggler,… There were cobblers patching the varieties of old shoes, tailors at work on garments whose luster had long disappeared, and regenerators of paper umbrellas, while another wove strips of rattan in great round and shockingly bad hats." [12] This was a specific and active description of the street life of Canton at that time. However, comparing this quote with the views of the albums, Hunter's description looks as if it is not enough.

The reader will find much more to appreciate in each picture beyond its inherent beauty. The picture "Making Foreign Shoes" by Puqua (35)is undoubtedly the earliest image of a Chinese making leather

shoes. The developing glass industry in Canton is illustrated by Puqua's "Turning Glass Fish Jar"(77) and Tingqua's "Turning Glass"(21)and "Blowing Glass"(25).Tingqua's "Watching peepshows"(56) perhaps is a earliest image record of this new matter.

Tingqua's "Selling Newspaper"(90,255) and "Pasting Newspaper" (161) recorded a very remarkable new cultural phenomenon in the streets of Canton. Since 1827, the English language *Canton Register* was published in Canton. Since 1833, *Dong xi yang kao mei yue tong ji zhuan* (*Eastern Western Monthly Magazine*),an early Chinese magazine in China, was also published in Canton. In the 1830s, the newspapers sold on the streets of Canton were probably these publications. The Chinese 新文(Xingwen)and 新文紙(Xingwenzhi)are free translations of English "news" and "newspaper", afterward the Chinese characters 新聞and新聞紙(also reading as Xingwen and Xingwenzhi)were used. As with this example, we believe that those in the fields of social, economic and cultural history, will find new information in these images, beyond their use in the general study of Chinese export paintings.

Chinese export paintings always display some subjects that are observable, describable, and characteristic of certain parts of Chinese history and culture. Their special attraction is perhaps stronger today than when they were first produced, still holding our gaze and wanting us to know more. In addition to the artist's level of competence we are drawn to know more about their historical and cultural significance. They serve as a special medium that allows West-erners to better understand China.

While Chinese traditional culture was being introduced to Europe and America, the Westerners were perceiving that country in more depth from the enormous quantities of export arts and crafts introduced through the China trade. The effects of Chinese export paintings can not be underestimated because they are visual, conspicuous, and very comprehensive in subject. The Westerners who acquired these albums and individuals works of art collected, displayed and distributed them throughout Europe and America. Such imformation was so broad, vivid and picturesque that seeing only this album is enough to suggest the wonder such works would bring. It is obvious that China trade paintings were effective in presenting Chinese images to the West before photography was transmitted into China. As for some subjects, such as the 360 professions, even photography would never be able to leave a more thorough or integrated record of such historical importance.

Shijian Huang and William R. Sargent
August, 1999.

1. For this Kind of Chinese export paintings, the European and American gave other names, such as traders, peddlers and artisans, streets trades, daily live, Chinese customs, etc. It seems that the westerners who collected, managed or studied these paintings at that time and at present did not know the saying "360 professions" in China.

2. About Suzhou woodcut, cf. Shigeru Aoki and Mitsuhi ro Kobayashi (supervised and edited), *The Exhibition of Chinese Foreign Style Paintings——the Pictures, Woodcuts and Illustrations from the End of Ming to the Qing Time*, Municipal-run International Woodcut Museum, 1995, ill. 375-411. Xiaoye Mo, "The Influence of Western Paintings Seen on the SuxhouWoodcut in Qianlong Period" , Shijian Huang (ed.), *On the Communication between Chinese and the West*, Shanghai Literature and Art Press, 1998, pp.215—229.

3. Cf. Craig Clunas, *Chinese Export Watercolours*, Victoria and Albert Museum, 1984, p.10.

4. The "rice paper" in fact was one kind of paper made of "tong cao" (Aralia papyrifira), it could be earlier read in John Francis Davis' *The Chinese: A General Description of the Empire of China and Its Inhabitants*, New York, 1836,rep.1972,p.15.cf.Craig Clunas, *Chinese Export Watercolours*, Victoria and Albert Museum, 1984, pp.80—81.

5. S.W.Williams had described this kind of paper and how it was suitable to absorb in colors owing to its surface configuration.cf. Williams' *Middle Kingdom*, London,

1848, Vol.II, P.175.

6. There was a document entitled"Concerning European Ship and Trade to Canton by a Native Chinese, Translated from the Original M.S." with a taxes table of imports and exports in Robert Morrison, *Notes concerning China and the Port of Canton, Also a Narrative of the Affair of the English Frigate Topaze, 1821－1822. with Remarks on Homicides, and an Account of the Fire of Canton*, Malacca, 1823, pp.39—49. One of the items was "洋顔料 Yaong-en-lew"(foreign paints).

7. Old Nick, *La Chine Ouverte*, Paris, 1845,p.58.

8. Williams, vol.II,p.175.

9. Osmand Tiffany, *The Canton Chinese, or the American's Sojourn in the Celestial Empire*, Boston & Cambridge:James Munroe and Co., 1849, p.83.

10. There was a Chinese inscription on the middle horizontal board in one of pictures of the so-called "Tingqua Studio" .At the end of the inscription, we can see six Chinese characters 俊卿四兄雅屬 (jun-qing -si-xong-ya-shu),that means "to the fourth elder brother", so we can make sure that Tingqua was the fourth in Guan's brothers. Junqing should be Tingqua's secondary formal name.

11. G.H.Mason was a English soldier stayed in Madras in India, he visited Canton in 1790 and bought a set of Puqua's gouaches there. After returning England, he published an album, *The Costumes of China*, in 1800, but Puqua's original works were changed as stipple engraved plates by W.Miller.However the original types were apparently preserved, and each picture was with the words "Pu Qua, Canton, Delin" at its left lower corner. cf. George H. Mason, *The Customs of China*, London, 1800 Carl L. Crossman, *The Decorative Arts of the China Trade: Paintings, Furnishings and Exotic Curiosities*, Antique Collectors' Club, Suffolk, England, 1991, p.185.

12. William C. Hunter, *Bits of Old China*, London, 1855; rep. Taipei, 1966,p.13.

蒲呱水粉畫一百幅

100 GOUACHES BY PUQUA

扇　約1850年
中國外銷品
埃絲特·奧爾德姆女士捐贈

Fan　c.1850
Chinese Export Fan
Gift of Miss Esther Oldham

補瓷碗　1800年
蒲呱　點雕畫
採自梅森《中國服裝》，倫敦，1800年

Patching Porcelain Bowl, 1800
Puqua, Stipple Engravings
From G. H. Mason's *The Costumes of China*, London, 1800

A Pork Peddler

賣豬肉

一副凳頭一把刀
外洋豬肉價錢高
肋條要把豬蹄搭
利市順風半是毛

——

童謙孟

十九世紀中國市井風情

4

賣缸瓦

An Earthenware

A Duster Peddler 　賣鷄毛掃

竹枝詞

雞毛作掃售城鄉
咸愛輕靈用景忙
長短配成藤竹柄
漆膠線扎制精良

佚名

十九世紀中國市井風情

6

賣魚

A Fish Monger

竹枝詞

豪門漫詡牛心炙
詞客休誇鴨腳羹
屈指菊花天氣近
小鑼響處賣魚生

江仲瑜

三百六十行 360 PROFESSION

A Performing Juggling

演大戲法

竹枝詞

香車寶馬日闐闐
百戲棚開瓦廠前
一棒鼓聲和笑語
無風人聚看場園

———

方元鵾

賣老鼠藥

A Rat Poison Seller

竹枝詞

樹邊小石祈年社
擊鼓吹螺賽伯公
薰鼠若能供薦福
伯公當保一年豐

——趙希璜

三百六十行 360 PROFESSION

A Silkworm Attendant　　　　　看蠶

竹枝詞

采桑陌上看名姝
綠苑丹黃入畫圖
待得繭成春已去
切教珍重繡羅襦

徐乾學

十九世紀中國市井風情

10

找錢

A Man Giving Change of Money

竹枝詞

百　　近　通　物
十　　來　街　價
銀　　海　除　低
錢　　舶　陌　昂
中　　殊　市　心
灌　　多　行　倒
鉛　　詐　錢　顛

——
陳文瑞

三百六十行 360 PROFESSION

A Modeler Making an Immortal Statue   塑神像

僧旗佛傘下層層
寶座高燒無盡燈
寫有妙香裝法像
布施連日滿龍興

竹枝詞

郭
麟

澆燭 　　　　　　　　　　　　　　　　A Candle Maker

竹枝詞

一支蓮炬一樓臺
仿佛燈輪西域里
自有銀花火樹開
不須秉燭夜游來

——佚名

十九世紀中國市井風情

整弓箭

A Bow and Arrow Maker

竹枝詞

椎髻如螺與額齊
弓刀常愛手中攔
往來有信惟傳箭
事到狐疑侭割雞

——

任兆麓

三百六十行 360 PROFESSIONS

做鞭杆

A Whip and Rod Maker

A Cobbler

補鞋

竹枝詞

脂紅粉白出嬌娃
滿市燒豬壓斷街
金字招牌標識好
新花時樣女娘鞋

彭玉麟

十九世紀中國市井風情

16

賣豆腐

A Bean Curd Peddler

竹枝詞

牽斷風箱開五更
磨來豆腐明朝賣
前街便有水淋聲
廳尾門頭月尚明

——童謙孟

三百六十行 360 PROFESSION

十九世紀中國市井風情

A Making Braid Lady   打辮綫

17

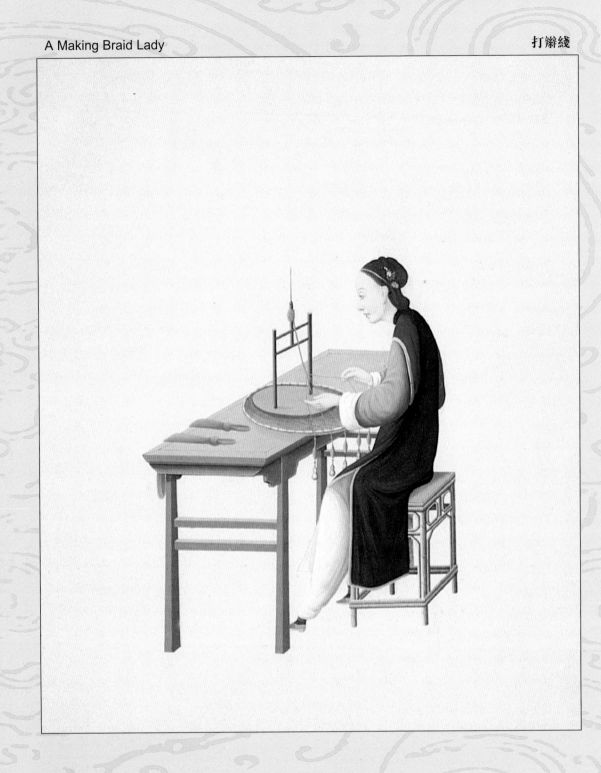

十九世紀中國市井風情

18

賣風爐

A Charcoal Stove Peddler

百凡爐包故田換月
陰不爛不列不碳請遇
造招牌左記江爐正記

* 賣，原作買，逕改。

竹枝詞

夢殘酒渴五更時
憔悴燈前鬢欲絲
一具風爐兩茶碗
生涯猶有故人知

——

馮敏昌

Making Liquor

造酒

十九世紀中國市井風情

19

竹枝詞

寶漢名寮小北張
客朋從此樂壺觴
肥魚大酒朝朝醉
誰奠芳魂廿四娘

——鄧絢裳

十九世紀中國市井風情

山水梅湯

A Plum Juice Vendor

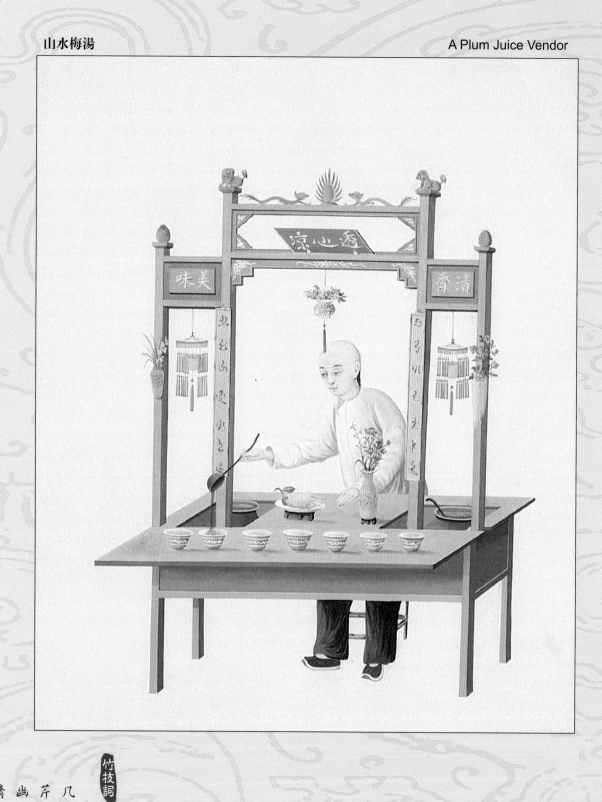

 竹枝詞

清氣宜湯豌豆尖
幽香配酒藜蒿梗
芹芽脆逗荻芽鮮
幾種園蔬美又廉

——
葉調元

A Repairman for Sharpening Knives   削刀

弄雀

十九世紀中國市井風情

22

竹枝詞

見人也會噴燒茶
紅嘴綠毛心更巧
隴外何容獨自誇
山中鸚鵡艷如花

任兆麓

三百六十行 360 PROFESSION

十九世紀中國市井風情

A Painter

寫畫

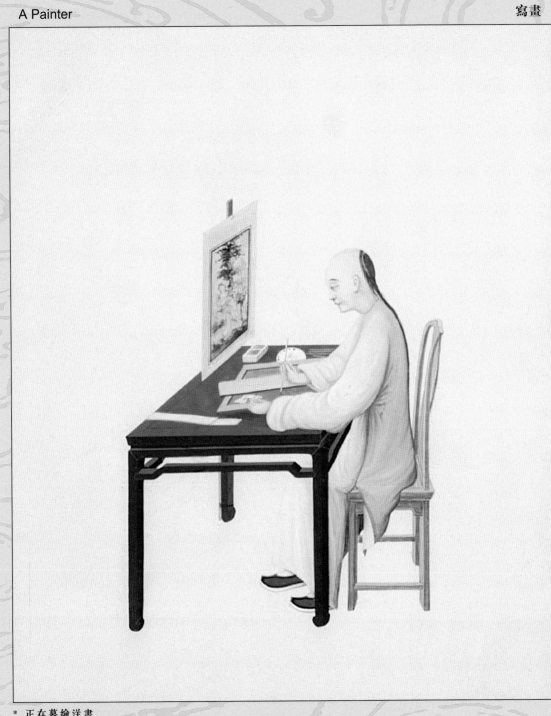

* 正在摹繪洋畫。

* Just copying a western painting.

車夫

A Wheelbarrow Pusher

十九世紀中國市井風情

24

竹枝詞

碾碾車輪是阿心
幾回思寄白頭吟
雪峰井底絲三丈
不及龍淵潭水深

——馬壽穀

十九世紀中國市井風情

A Chinaware Repairman

補瓷缸

補瓷缸

十九世紀中國市井風情

26

趕豬郎

A Man Driving a Pig (To Market)

A Peddler Selling Towel Purse　　　　　　賣手巾袋

竹枝詞

嬌小綠窗一段春
桃花菜子可憐人
眼波眉暈聰明甚
學得桃花繡手巾

彭淑

整架

A Picture Frame Maker

* 整治安放畫頁或像片的框架。

十九世紀中國市井風情

A Hat Weaver　　　　　　　　　　　織帽

竹枝詞

鄰女織紗儂織葵
休嫌手拙作工遲
蒲葵葉葉裁明月
三五團圓不後時

——黎昀

三百六十行 360 PROFESSIONS

捶金箔

Hammering Gold Foil

十九世紀中國市井風情

Mounting Paper Fan "Face"

裱扇面

城廂扇館遍東西
花樣元多摺疊齊
聞道漢陽行市好
連宵工作到鳴雞

竹枝詞

高小雲

十九世紀中國市井風情

32

賣豆腐花　　　　　　　　　　　　　　A Bean Curd Jelly Peddler

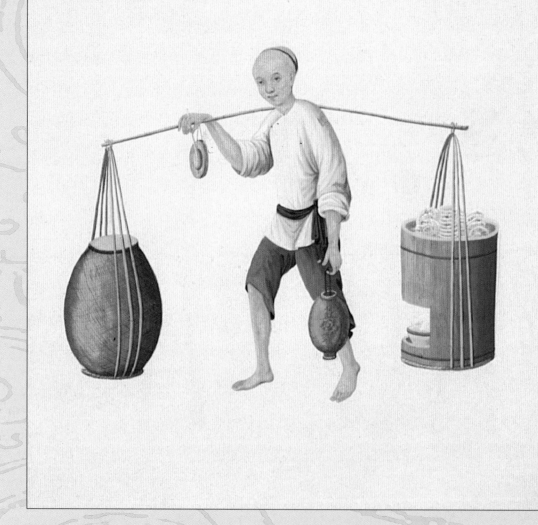

竹枝詞

乞巧更闌撤果瓜
睡酣紅日上窗紗
夢中鑼子東丁響
恨煞街頭豆腐花

陳其藻

A Tailor

裁縫

成衣術業有專攻
男子紛紛代女工
鬧煞閨中針刺手
不須刀尺學裁縫

——

童謙孟

十九世紀中國市井風情

鑽珠

A Jeweler

34

* The original meaning of the Chinese title is "drilling pearl".

竹枝詞

珠海珠娘珠翠樓
珠光月色一般秋
阿娘見說珍珠好
喚作珠兒當兆頭

——梁榮鎏

十九世紀中國市井風情

A Floss-silk Peddler

賣絨綫

竹枝詞

排當真成錦一窩
妙偷鴛杼勝鸞梭
何須更向天孫乞
只覺閨中巧更多

——汪琇

十九世紀中國市井風情

36

賣茨菰

An Arrowhead Root Peddler

竹枝詞

不　更　一　水
生　比　月　萍
綠　梧　圓　廣
葉　桐　成　育
結　能　一　似
明　報　個　慈
珠　閏　菰　姑

—
陳坤

Making Foreign Shoes

整番鞋

* 製作皮鞋。可見當時皮鞋已傳入中國。
* Foreign shoes means leather shoes. So it had been spread into China.

竹枝詞

鬢盤委墮鬢如雲
宽袖蠻靴襯布裙
妝束工趨時世樣
女兒還喜演英文

——

戴達士

整煙筒斗   Making Tobacco Pipe

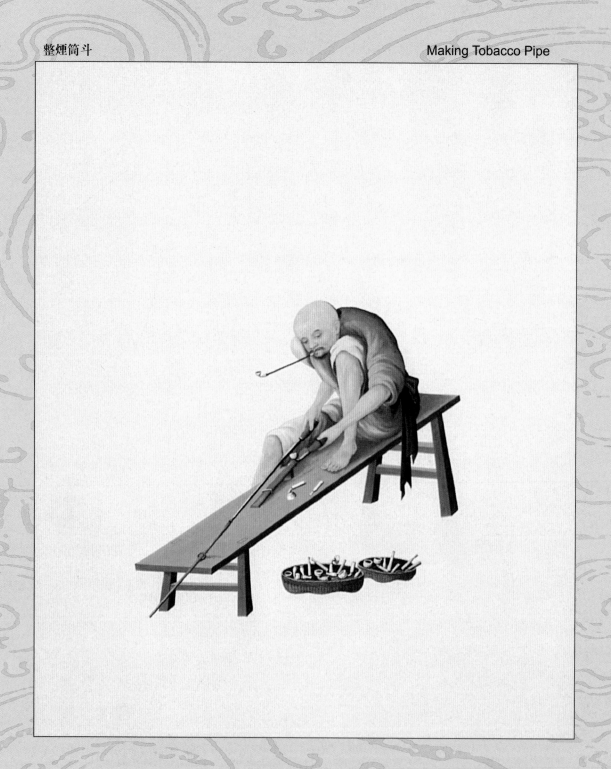

十九世紀中國市井風情

A Cat Peddler

賣貓

39

竹枝詞

不為迎貓祀虎忙
吹螺打鼓鬧山莊
几梳蕉芋黃于酒
蟻祖祠前夜進香

——陶元藻

二百六十行 360 PROFESSIONS

十九世紀中國市井風情

點秤

Making Scale

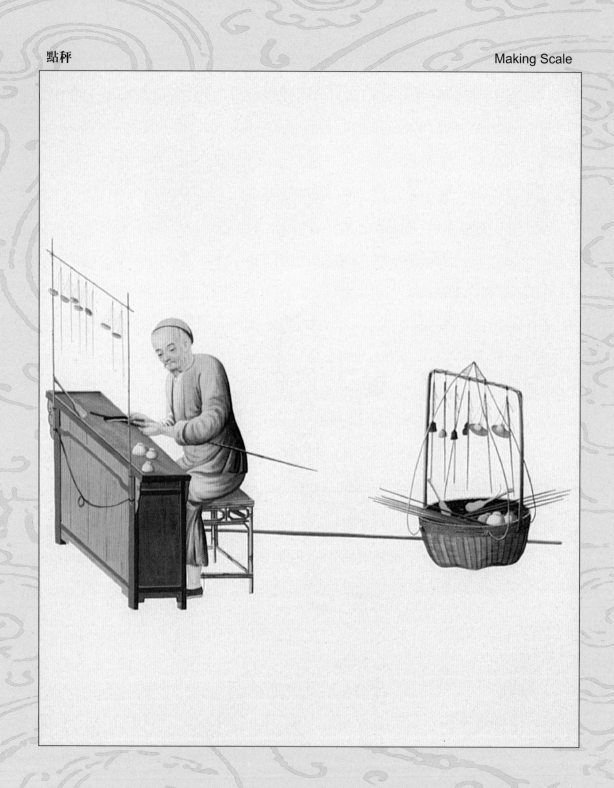

點秤

Making Scale

A Broom Peddler

賣掃把

竹枝詞

竹帚除塵敢告勞
新書喜字貼周遭
專門更要雙紅蔗
佇望年來節節高

——葉如圭

十九世紀中國市井風情

倒屎娘

A Woman Turning over Nightsoil

竹枝詞

挑柴賣芋復擔油
百十成群盡女流
北地此風從未見
耐勞婦女獨炎州

——焦和生

A Bird Hunter

彈雀

竹枝詞

野芋山姜雜土薯
田螺坦蜆軟蝦蓎
只須一味禾花雀
不數珠江馬鱭魚

——

胡
鶴

十九世紀中國市井風情

44

整帽

Making Hat

竹枝詞

莫帽好麥
把成將草
些親燈挑
錢手下齊
付交績滿
酒郎新屋
家賣麻又

——李克芃

Spinning Silk

解絲

十九世紀中國市井風情

竹枝詞

荔枝灣畔水環村
儂日繰絲郎灌園
二月芥蘭三月蒜
擔頭侵曉入西門

——利普

十九世紀中國市井風情

46

踩鼓

Repairing Drum

* 踩，廣州方言用字，讀若 cai（入聲）。從畫面看，當是修理鼓。

三百六十行 360 PROFESSION

十九世紀中國市井風情

Making Trunk 整夾萬

47

* 夾萬，廣州方言，意爲存放金錢的保險櫃。

鏨鎖花

Chiseling Design on Locks

鏨鎖花

三百六十行 360 PROFESSION

十九世紀中國市井風情

A Silversmith

打銀

竹枝詞

梳妝從儉洗鉛華
買串銀絲綰鬢丫
若得香魂同不死
一生長伴素馨花

紫藤女史

三百六十行 360 PROFESSIONS

十九世紀中國市井風情

箍桶　　　　　　　　　　　　　　　　　　　　　　　　Repairing Bucket

Mending by Darning

織補

竹枝詞

砧杵聲停客未歸
手中針線認依稀
當街耐冷縫窮婦
但爲他人補舊衣

佚名

十九世紀中國市井風情

52

打磨

A Stone Mason Making Millstone

竹枝詞

麥葉蠶肥客可餐
棟花鱔熟子盈盤
家家鍛磨聲初歇
四月江村有薄寒

——沈明臣

A Flower Peddler 賣花

竹枝詞

花市柵頭花聚處
斑斕五色各盈筐
花籃載去沿街賣
散作千家繡閣香

——
張維屏

唱獨腳戲　　　　　　　　　　　　　　A Monodrama Player

十九世紀中國市井風情

54

竹枝詞

小戲開場獨腳班
骨丟誰識巧機關
一身妙盡絲兼肉
妒殺濠州十不閒

——李聲振

A Chicken and Duck Peddler

賣雞鴨

十九世紀中國市井風情

竹枝詞

一籠雞鴨一籠鵝
隨帶糠團忘若何
豈是飢禽須飽飼
賺人應在秤頭多

——童謙孟

十九世紀中國市井風情

56

舞馬騮

A Monkey Trainer

* 馬騮，廣州方言，讀若ma-lau，意爲猴。

竹枝詞

近來耍戲更新鮮
教法能將富類傳
猴子狗熊頑棍棒
雀兒老鼠打秋千

——葉調元

十九世紀中國市井風情

A Lacquerware Painter with Gold Color

描金漆器

竹枝詞

金漆磨礱鏡不如
光華何止慶豐車
游龍一瞥驚雷過
不使纖塵動九衢

——李寶淦

十九世紀中國市井風情

補鑊

A Blacksmith Patching Cooker

十九世紀中國市井風情

A Lady Weaver

織布

竹枝詞

軋軋鳴機織布忙

織紗成布潔于霜

果真布出家機好

妾意郎情縷共長

陳坤

十九世紀中國市井風情

磨麵

A Miller Milling Flour

竹枝詞

重羅細麵淨于楷
餺飥饅頭列滿街
薄餅自來從上揭
怕人錯認是招牌

——李于璜

An Incense Peddler

賣香

黃瑞
明香

竹枝詞

宮蓮東岳竹蓮庵
香火因緣結兩龕
不解村姑多少事
拜餘佛祖拜伽藍

胡曦

十九世紀中國市井風情

車煙桿

Making Tobacco Pipe

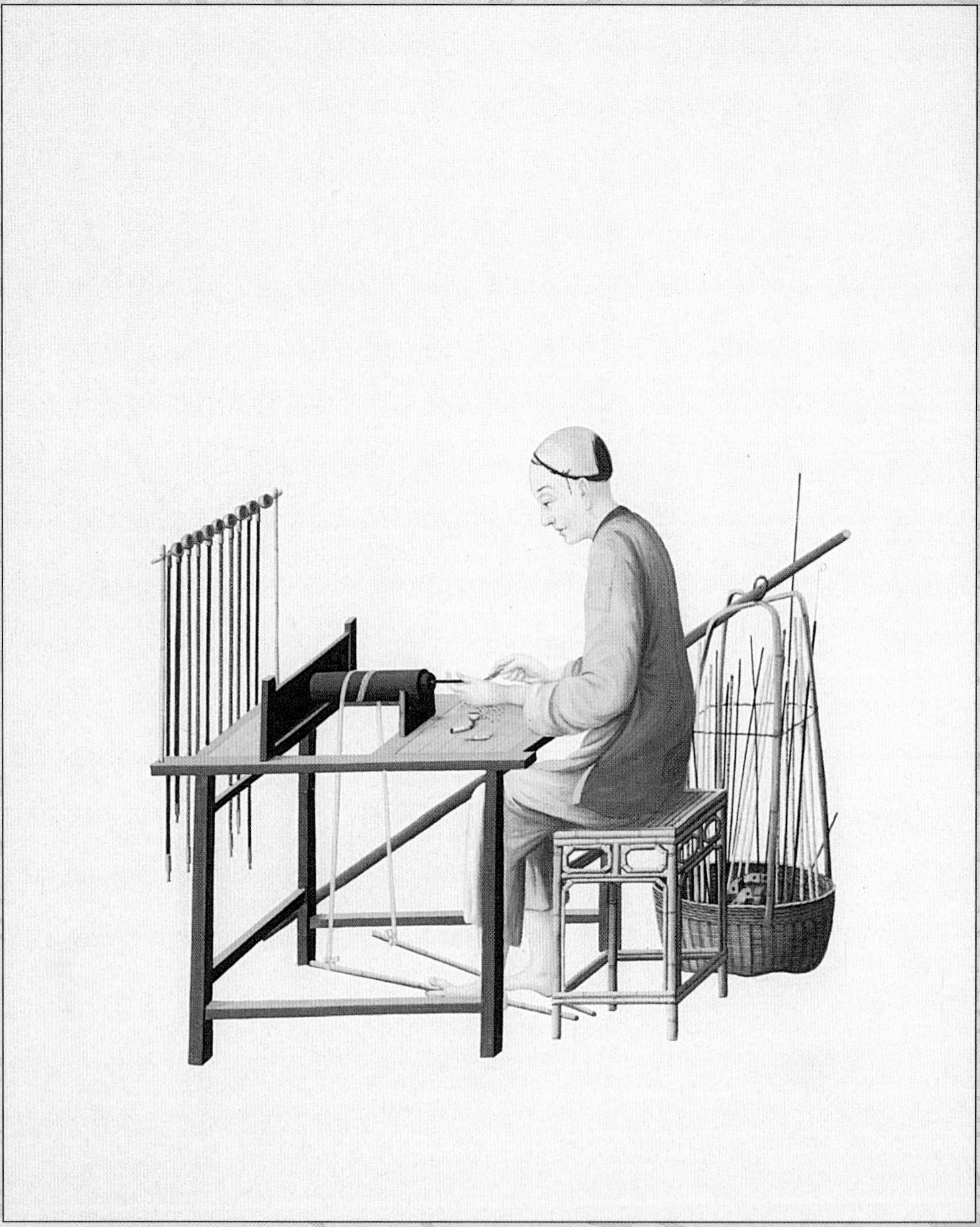

竹枝詞

煙袋名稱侍衛帶
虎皮箸箬正時裝
咀須翡翠方招眼
玉手高擎玳瑚光

——張子秋

三百六十行 360 PROFESSION

A Mason Chiseling Stone

鑿石

竹枝詞

鑿石題詩古蘚封
水天吟嘯欲驚龍
亂山樹入秋空碧
斜日來聽海閣鐘

潘飛聲

三百六十行 360 PROFESSIONS

十九世紀中國市井風情

64

賣假藥　　　　　　　　　　　　　　　　A Fake Medicine Peddler

竹枝詞

費盡心機混假真
百般奇巧鬥鮮新
名爲骨操時時摔
慣向街頭騙傻人

——得碩亭

三百六十行 360 PROFESSION

A Traveling Physician Specializing in Hemorrhoids

修養

* 當時 "修養" 一詞有 "治療" 的含義。參見頁 125 藏包先生。

十九世紀中國市井風情

66

賣梳篦

A Comb Peddler

竹枝詞

梳篦銷場重口才
各人口岸各人開
年年只有張公道
別個未來他就來

——劉師亮

三百六十行 360 PROFESSION

A Oil Painter

油漆

竹枝詞

山魈木魅并川狐
石鏡瑩瑩當禹圖
漆縱能遮法照
豈防山下有明湖

——王象春

十九世紀中國市井風情

淘沙

Panning Sand

十九世紀中國市井風情

A Sandal Maker　　　　　　釘屐

竹枝詞

八月炎荒秋未涼
風流群屐少年場
高樓館中飲美酒
高梘艇里挾名娼

——鮑鉁

整天平

A Precision Balance Maker

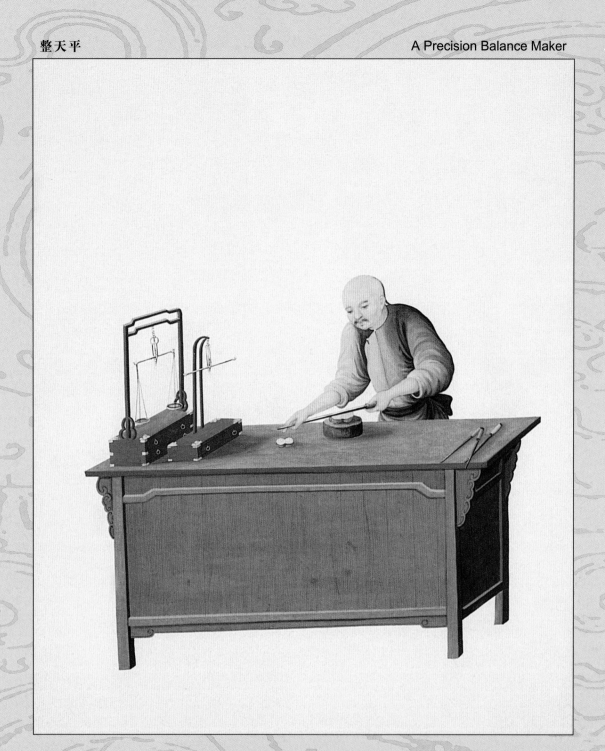

十九世紀中國市井風情

Shaving Tobacco Leaves　　　　　　　　　　刨煙

71

竹枝詞

誰栽煙草抵桑麻
浪說收成到倍誇
別有相思消不得
一燈紅映米囊花

*
米囊花即罌粟花。

——余茂

十九世紀中國市井風情

補遮

An Umbrella Repairman

* 廣州方言，遮即傘。

竹枝詞

好送行雲伴客裝
晴遮炎日陰遮雨
烏油傘蓋製精良
玉骨玲瓏妙翁張

方鼎銳

三百六十行 360 PROFESSION

Spinning Ramie Thread

織麻

竹枝詞

深閨會製踏春衣
又績新麻掩竹扉
儂會拋梭郎莫笑
織來爭似女人機

——袁俞枌

絞花

Twisting Cotton

竹枝詞

春風無地不桑麻
閒種山田四五家
竟日工夫拋不得
繰車鳴處紡棉花

趙棨正

Entertaining Dragon Boat Model

舞旱龍

竹枝詞

買舟同日擲金錢
爆竹聲中笑語傳
指點五仙門外水
彩旗畫鼓鬥龍船

——江仲瑜

賣羅斗

A Bamboo Baskets Peddler

A Palm Leaf Fan Peddler

賣葵扇

竹枝詞

五里亭連中道亭
春風一路草青青
送郎賣扇羊城去
莫到花田戀素馨

——
陳其藻

十九世紀中國市井風情

打薄餅

Beating Thin Pan-cake

竹枝詞

上巳清明取次過
南關北郭雨滂沱
壚頭薄餅煙還暖
到處人家買驚多

——
蕭同寅

三百六十行 360 PROFESSION

Turning Glass Fish Jar

車魚缸

竹枝詞

堂皇虛敞撤門窗
雁齒層層基壘石砠
四角短檐天井窄
階心恰放變魚缸

＊
金魚謂之變魚

——
謝階樹

十
九
世
紀
中
國
市
井
風
情

80

閘夫

A Night Watchman

竹枝詞

多因更點不曾敲
聽鼓出城常失曉
覓向遙村及近郊
花豬黃犬競充庖

陳文瑞

三百六十行 360 PROFESSION

Writing on Lantern

寫燈籠

竹枝詞

頭號風箏放用繩
四郊角逐鬧青輕
既懸燈籠夜未點
還挂鷂簧天半鳴

——
張延章

十九世紀中國市井風情

82

做箱

Making Chest

竹枝詞

生儿莫道在村莊
也要經書念几行
縮個木箱提簍飯
山神廟里是學堂

——
彭淑

三百六十行 360 PROFESSION

十九世紀中國市井風情

A Barber

剃頭

竹枝詞

對鏡晨妝鬖似蓬
首無膏沐暑為容
煩君理就青絲鬢
擁首佳人定愛濃

羅四峰

三百六十行 360 PROFESSIONS

十九世紀中國市井風情

梭綫

Making Thread by Twisting Yarn Together

竹枝詞

徹夜聲勤是紡車
百姿橋畔移舟宿
家家只紡木棉紗
也種柔桑也種麻

林中麒

三百六十行 360 PROFESSION

十九世紀中國市井風情

Embroidering Flower 繡花

竹枝詞

唱罷南音晝正長
拈針微笑繡鴛鴦
阿儂家住蓮花井
嫁得檀郎似六郎

—
徐錫瓚

十九世紀中國市井風情

打錫

A Tinsmith

竹枝詞

沈郎煎錫白於銀
翻出壺天異樣新
料理候湯點春茗
不須陽羨問甕春

——吳萃恩

三百六十行 360 PROFESSIONS

Dumpling Peddler

賣扁食

竹枝詞

餛飩擔子市街挑
聞有筒聲橐橐敲
敲暖鄉村紅杈路
依稀風景祝都橋

童謙孟

拆字

A Fortune Teller

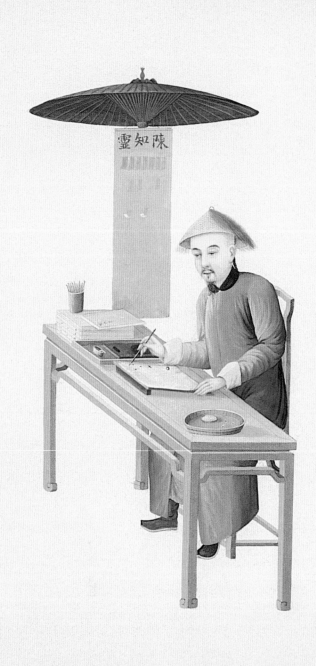

* To tell fortune by analyzing the component part of a Chinese character written by the customer.

竹枝詞

學數談星各隱占
偏旁字拆減還添
心馳商賈工農外
且設君平卜肆帘

——陳文瑞

A Fur Peddler

賣皮草

竹枝詞

皮褲山綢物價諧
兔肩鹿尾市門排
一條軟繡差堪擬
深夜籠燈買賣街

——吳錫麟

整扇骨

Making Fan's Bone

竹枝詞

真棕扇甲象牙鑲
新樣全描綠間黃
破尾孤燈兩枝筆
郎描蘇武妾王嬌

——陳其藻

三百六十行 360 PROFESSION

A Mutton Peddler

賣羊肉

竹枝詞

山羊香脆土羊肥
褐兔胸脮白兔皮
梨落忽聞池水響
更彎筍弩射香狸

謝階樹

榨玉香

A "Jade" Incense Maker

十九世紀中國市井風情

A Pickled Vegetable Peddler

賣鹹菜

竹枝詞

貨不論鮮只要堅
暴鹹貨物賽冰鮮
攤頭嘖嘖向人贊
江貨來非蟹浦船

—— 童謙孟

賣席

A Mat Peddler

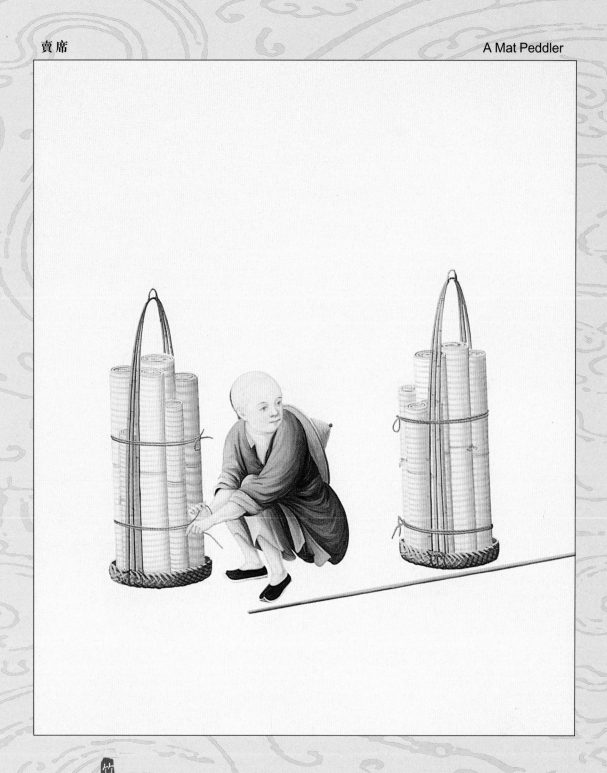

竹枝詞

街名一半店名呼
蘆席稀稀草紙粗
一事令人惆悵甚
美人街上美人無

葉調元

十九世紀中國市井風情

A Magician   使法

＊ 使法，即施法變魔術之意。

编麻   Making Hemp

* 编，原作邊，當是音近而俗借。

Selling Soybean Milk

賣漿

竹枝詞

豆腐方方似截肪
香乾名數盂家揚
汁能滋養勝牛乳
無怪街頭多賣漿

—— 馮文洵

十九世紀中國市井風情

賣雀　　　　　　　　　　　　　　　Selling Bird

鵪鶉能鬥鴿能飛
竹葉青青翠羽微
好向陶莊捕黃雀
披綿勝似野雞肥

孫圃

三百六十行 360 PROFESSION

Selling Vegetable

賣菜

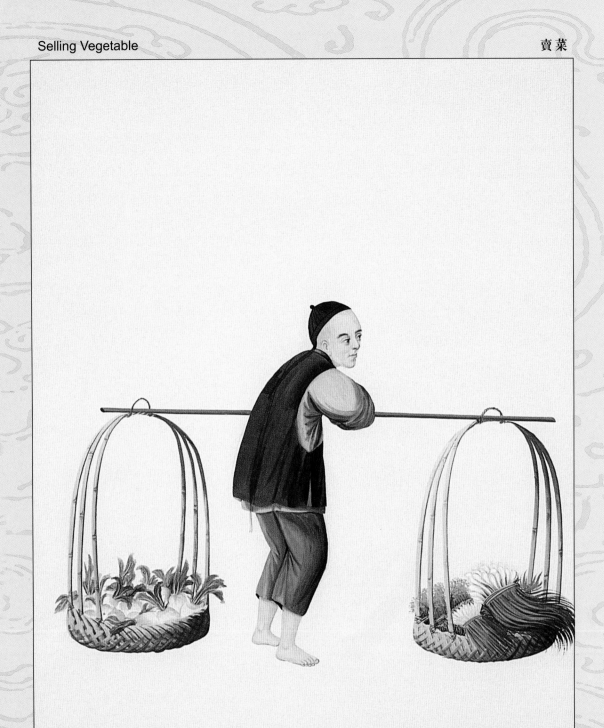

竹枝詞

侵晨挑菜出芳村
綠葉黃花白雪根
可怪一雙黃蛺蝶
擔頭追逐入西門

鄧鳳樞

十九世紀中國市井風情

苦煉修行

A Penitential Buddhist Monk

* 以自我傷害表示虔誠的苦行僧。

A Snake Medicine Peddler　　　　　　　　　　　賣蛇藥

彈棉花

Fluffing Cotton Filler

竹枝詞

棉花街里白漫漫
誰把孤弦竟日彈
彈到落花流水處
滿身風雪不知寒

——韓珠船

庭呱綫描畫三百六十幅

360 INK DRAWINGS BY TINGQUA

水果酒盆　約1788年
中國外銷瓷器
小哈里・彼得斯捐贈

Punch Bowl　c.1788
Chinese Export Porcelain
Gift of Miss Esther of Mr. Harry T. Peters, Jr.

庭呱自畫像
1854年　綫描畫
見于"咸豐四年吉日立"畫册

Tingqua, Self-portrait
1854　Ink-drawing
From an Album of Tingqua Studio

十九世紀中國市井風情

Sifting Tea　　　　　　　　　　　　　篩茶

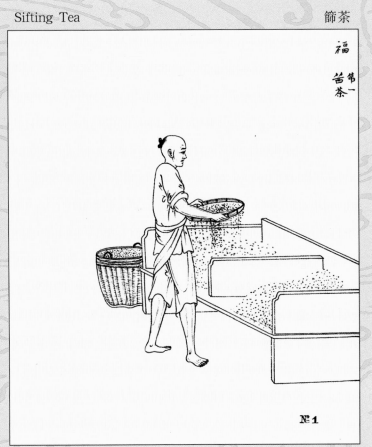

№ 1

＊篩，原作笹，俗字。

竹枝詞

雨前幾日苬新芽
山北山南唱采茶
采得滿籃兼滿袖
小姑雙鬢壓梨花

——張其禄

Trampling Tea　　　　　　　　　　　　踩茶

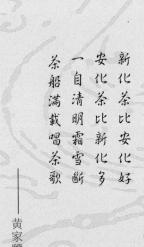

竹枝詞

新化茶比安化好
安化茶比新化多
一自清明霜雪斷
茶船滿載唱茶歌

——黃家驥

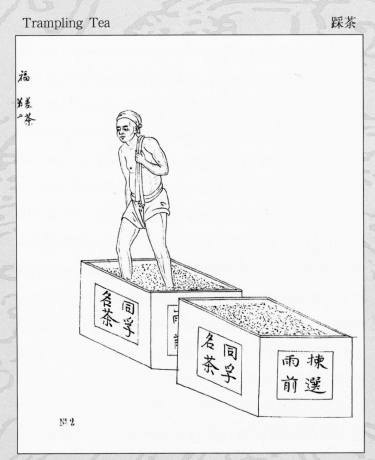

№ 2

踩，原作差，當是音近而俗借。

十九世紀中國市井風情

竹枝詞

百行生意近俱淡
惟有茶林獨擁擠
不愛茶新愛茶舊
座中佳客真品題

——徐朗軒

搓茶　　　　Grinding Tea (with fingers)

福
第三
搓茶

№3

曬茶　　　　Drying Tea (under the sun)

福
第四
曬茶

№4

Monkey Picking Tea　　　　　　　　　　猴子采茶

* 茶農中常有讓猴子攀到山崖上采取珍貴岩茶的説法。

Cutting Tea　　　　　　斬茶

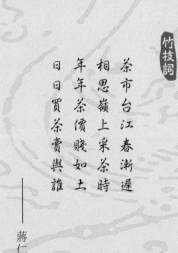

竹枝詞

茶市台江春漸遲
相思嶺上采茶時
年年茶價賤如土
日日買茶賣與誰

——蔣仁

十九世紀中國市井風情

渡茶　　　　　　　　　Ferrying Tea

福渡茶第七

№ 7

竹枝詞

古墓為田長素馨
素馨斜外草青青
采茶人唱花田曲
舟外橋邊隔樹聽

——李環浦

裝茶　　　　　　　　　Packing Tea

福裝茶第八

№ 8

竹枝詞

商販頻來物價賒
山中茗味最堪嘉
紫雲宮外香氛繞
滿市紅茶與白茶

——王昌南

三百六十行 360 PROFESSIONS

Pestling Tea　　　　　　　　　　　　春茶

福第宗九茶

№ 9

* 舂，原作宗，當是音近而俗借。

Selecting Tea　　　　　　　　　　　　揀茶

竹枝詞

自小從娘學揀茶
強伸纖手摘春芽
昨朝偶染商人指
羞過河南第幾家

——紫藤女史

福第揀十茶

10

試茶 Testing Tea

竹枝詞

一紙壚中火候誇
雨前雨後辨新芽
蓮花荇共鳴爬井
汲得清泉好試茶

——佚名

110

托茶 Carrying Tea (on the shoulder)

三百六十行 360 PROFESSION

Classifying Tea

分茶

竹枝詞

青崖二月雨濛濛
只采仙芽不解烘
搜遍御茶園里種
嫩香分里小筠籠

——杭世駿

福
分茶

13

Making Tea Cake

整茶餅

福
整茶餅
十四

14

十九世紀中國市井風情

號茶箱　　　　　　　　　　　　Numbering Tea Chest

福號茶箱 十五

15

裝箱　　　　　　　　　　　Packing Tea

福裝箱 十六

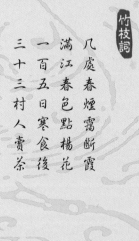

16

竹枝詞

几處春煙靄斷霞

滿江春色點楊花

一百五日寒食後

三十三村人賣茶

——胡鶴

三百六十行 360 PROFESSION

十九世紀中國市井風情

Stir-drying Tea 炒茶

福
炒.十
茶　七

17

竹枝詞

最難忘處三春事
楊柳參差蝴蝶忙
摘蕙滿山裙帶綠
焙茶十里水泉香

——陳維崧

Sprinkling Tea 灑水

福
灑.十
水　八

18

十九世紀中國市井風情

114

流民婦　　　　　　　　　　　　　　　Vagrant Woman

19

* 原題如此。據畫面，與題目不切，當有誤。

打錫器　　　　　　　　Hammering Tin Ware

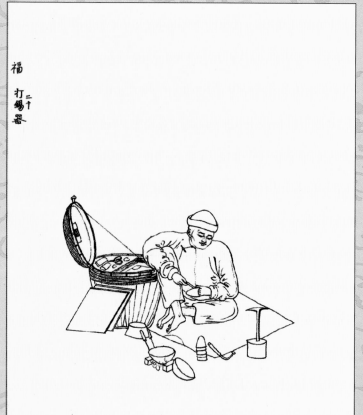

竹枝詞

錫器高橋葉製佳
百年不壞舊招牌
製范技擅黃中理
畫牡丹居周浦街

——秦榮光

十九世紀中國市井風情

Turning Glass　　車玻璃

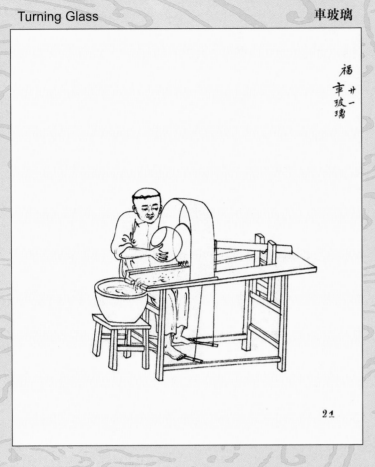

福
廿一
車玻璃

竹枝詞

龍游城郭碧玻璃
西望三峨曉黛滋
分取三江作明鏡
鏡中各自照蛾眉

——王士禎

21

115

Selling Bamboo Shoots　　賣竹笋

竹枝詞

編帘護竹竹成帘
筍到春時長嫩尖
舍北舍南都剝盡
那知苦竹老頭甜

——馬壽穀

福
賣竹笋
廿二

22

十九世紀中國市井風情

唱盲妹　　Singing Blind Sister

竹枝詞

羅綺叢中未解愁
洋錢輕擲買歌喉
琵琶卓杖深宵鬧
二八盲姑唱粵謳

——佚名

賣鐵什物　　Selling Iron Miscellaneous Goods

竹枝詞

杖凳肩乘鐵器多
釘頭鍋子日相磨
人家家具需收拾
特地呼來莫奈何

——定晉岩樵叟

三百六十行 360 PROFESSIONS

Blowing Glass　　　　　　　　　　吹玻璃

Selling Lin-Fu　　　　　　　　　賣靈符

* Lin-Fu: magic drawn by Taoist priests to invoke or expel
spirits and bring good or ill future.

十九世紀中國市井風情

118

賣風爐　　　　　　　　　　　　　Selling Wind Stove

竹枝詞

斫膾烹鮮說嫩珠
風流裙屐日無虛
消寒最是圍爐好
買盡橋邊百尾魚

——雪裏芭蕉館

鈒藥材　　　　　　　　　　　　　Cutting Herbs

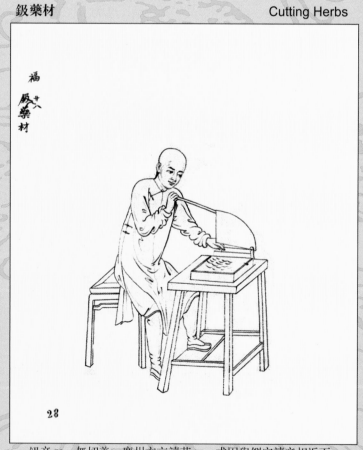

* 鈒音sa，無切義；廣州方言讀若za，或因與鍘字讀音相近而
俗借。

Covering Fish

罩魚

福
罩魚
廿九

竹枝詞

山如青黛水如羅
十里荔枝百頃荷
最是月明風靜夜
舟人齊唱摸魚歌

——阮祜

29

Selling Vegetable

賣菜

竹枝詞

蔬果青蔥載滿筐
慈菰苗短蔗竿長
輿中端坐人如玉
知是誰家新嫁娘

——錢塘漁

福
賣菜
三十

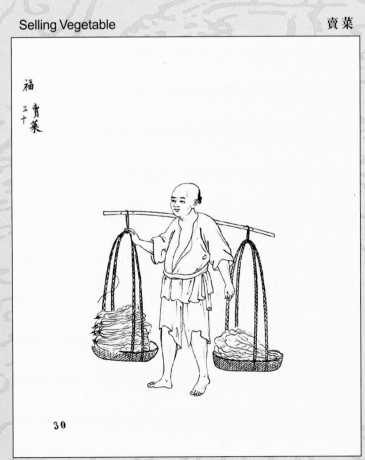

30

十九世紀中國市井風情

120

采桑　Picking Mulberry Leaves

竹枝詞

東山日赤雲氣昏
河姑勸我莫出門
持筐采得桑葉滿
直到阻雨溪南村

——宋裝

福
第卅一
抹桑

31

* It is for silkworm feeding.

秤桑　Weighing Mulberry Leaves

福
秤桑
第卅二

32

竹枝詞

青絲籠帶看蠶娘
兩岸人家齊采桑
繰得新絲何處賣
東新行販北新行

——張燕昌

十九世紀中國市井風情

Selling Salt　　　　　　　　　　　賣鹽

福

賣鹽

竹枝詞

越鹽如雪賽吳鹽
薯蕷初肥竹筍甜
何事眉山蘇太守
只將雙蟹較團尖

——汪廣洋

33

121

Selling Flute　　　　　　　　　　賣笛

福

賣笛

竹枝詞

楚腔激越少溫柔
解意雙鬟發妙謳
玉笛聽來都易辨
掃花折柳又藏舟

——張維屏

3

十九世紀中國市井風情

鎖鞋邊　　　　　　　　Sewing Shoes Sides

福廿五
賞難边

35

* 鎖，原作貟，或是書者的簡筆。

竹枝詞

襯出鴛鴦分外佳
匆匆繫個蓮舟樣
長短寬窄欠安排
赤腳無端遍著鞋

——王福坤

梳妝　　　　　　　　Hair-Dressing

竹枝詞

時新髻樣替梳頭
恰喜近身能會意
生小溫柔不解愁
衣裳楚楚悄風流

——陳坤

Selling Silkworm　　　　　　　　　　　　　　　賣蠶蟲

竹枝詞

村團社日喜晴和
銅鼓齊敲唱海歌
都道二年生計足
五收蠶繭兩收禾

——汪廣洋

Selling Silk　　　　　　　　　　　　　　　　賣絲

竹枝詞

洋船爭出是官商
十字門開向二洋
五絲八絲廣緞好
銀錢堆滿十三行

——屈大均

十九世紀中國市井風情

124

賣羊肉　　　　　　　　　　　Selling Mutton

竹枝詞

雷齋慈誕素成雙
口淡連朝興不降
配得福珍酒味厚
紅燒羊肉正開缸

——周斌

鹹水妹　　　　　　　　A Prostitute

竹枝詞

漁家燈上唱漁歌
一帶沙礁繞內河
阿妹近興鹹水調
聲聲押尾有兄哥

——張豐草

* 指稱生活在河道上的賣淫女。
* A term for the prostitute who lives at boat.

三百六十行 360 PROFESSIONS

十九世紀中國市井風情

Selling Porcelain 賣瓷器

松柴烈焰土坯燒
白地青花又淡描
仿古翻新誇樣好
官哥何許況宣窯

——陳文瑞

A Traveling Medical Doctor 藏包先生

賣絨綫　　　　　　　　　　Selling Knitting Wool

執字紙　Picking up Wastepaper with Chinese Characters

兒童盡日手提籃
遺字街頭次第拈
爲學蘇公符調水
循環教换綠紅籖

——陳其藻

三百六十行 360 PROFESSION

Shoveling Tobacco   鏟煙

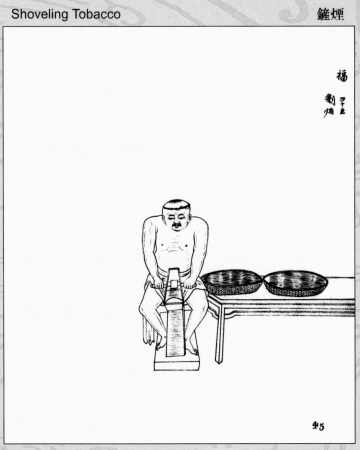

福
甲玉
劉烔

45

* 鏟，原作鐽，異體字。

Splitting Bamboo for Making Incense   破香竹

竹枝詞

竹公溪口水茫茫
溪上人家賽竹王
銅鼓蠻歌爭上日
竹林深處拜三郎

——王士禎

福
破香竹
甲午秋

46

十九世紀中國市井風情

128

賣鞋　　　　　　　　　Selling Shoes

釘屐　　　　　　　　　Nailing Sandal

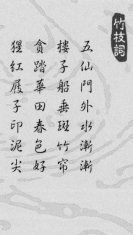

竹枝詞

五仙門外水漸漸
樓子船垂斑竹帘
貪踏華田春色好
猩紅屐子印泥尖

——潘兆鏗

十九世紀中國市井風情

A Master Predicting Fortune   算命先生

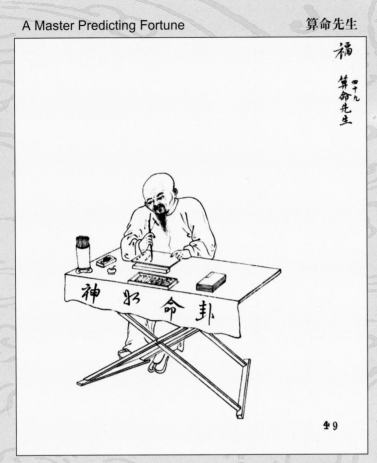

竹枝詞

山村祀竈果盤盤
爆竹聲停夜欲闌
小妹鄰家聽夜卦
多聞吉語暗心歡

——陳其藻

129

Selling Fish   賣魚

竹枝詞

珠海珠江是妾居
柳蔭停棹晚船初
水頭潮長賣花去
水尾潮來人賣魚

——任瑞隆

十九世紀中國市井風情

賣生熟漿　　Selling Raw and Cooked Soybean Milk

竹枝詞

荷鋤一隊轉坡坨
冷飯涼漿樹下多
開遍山花叫山鳥
鼓鑼處處唱山歌

——饒錫光

鑿石獅　　Carving Stone Lion

竹枝詞

元宵三五是佳期
都向衙門抱石獅
同作河東聲一吼
犬兒養出賣獅兒

*婦女抱石獅爲求子。

——王福坤

十九世紀中國市井風情

Drawing Flowers 寫花卉

福
五十三
寫花卉

53

竹枝詞

丹黃篔扇置妝臺
粉礁脂奩暫掃開
寒夜手僵呵凍寫
亂塗千點過墻梅

——胡曦

131

Spinning Cotton-Threads 紡紗

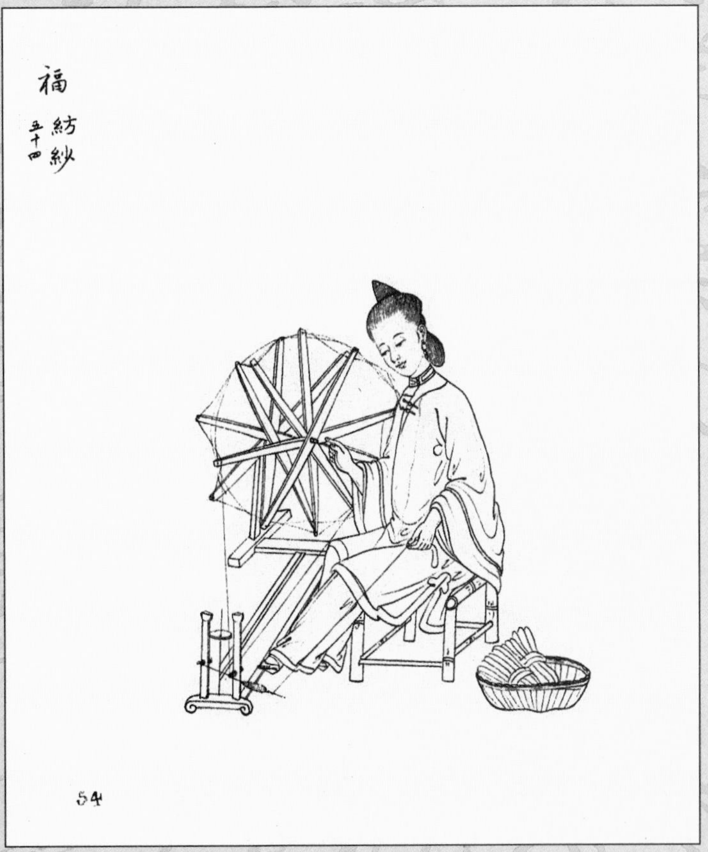

竹枝詞

米寨橋頭有水車
怳目村女紡棉紗
屏米河水歸樓門
樓下田禾分外嘉

——張捷成

福
五十四
紡紗

54

十
九
世
紀
中
國
市
井
風
情

132

賣茶壺　　　　　　　　　　　　　　　　　　Selling Tea Pot

福　五十五　賣茶壺

55

看西洋景　　　　　Watching Peepshows

福　五十六　看西洋景

56

竹枝詞

茶攤命棹西洋鏡
頑意多般集便河
真是賞心開散處
戲場各廟聚人多

——竹孫氏

十九世紀中國市井風情

Cutting Crystal　　　　　　�水晶

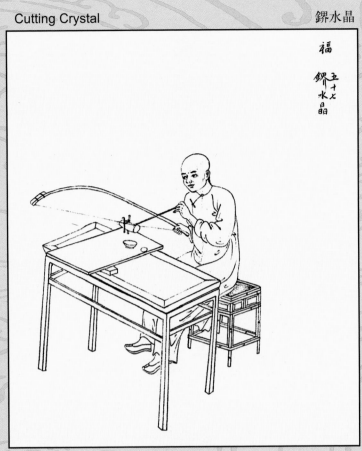

福
五十七
鎅水晶

* 鎅，廣州方言用字，讀若 gai，意爲裁割。

竹枝詞

香江接近五羊城
洋派由來説大英
蜑婦咭哩亦洋話
此間風氣令人驚

——胡子晋

Tanka Woman　　　　　　汲婦

福
蛋婦
五十八

58

* 蜑，原作蛋，當地以船爲家的水上居民。

* Tanka is local inhabitant living in the boat.

三百六十行 360 PROFESSIONS

十九世紀中國市井風情

賣臘味　　　　　Selling Preserved Meats

竹枝詞

賣臘回來摘臘忙
大姑娘喚小姑娘
攢攢簇簇勾分後
糝子肉洗瓢子觴

——胡道南

134

賣葵扇　　　　　Selling Palm-Leaf Fan

竹枝詞

淡淡衣裳淺淺妝
玉蘭花壓鬢雲香
春蔥搖曳蒲葵扇
斜溜秋波擲路郎

——何紹塘

Playing Tricks   弄把戲

竹枝詞

齲齲高擎玉一竿
竿頭旋轉舞冰盤
雖然不貯金莖露
已似銅仙掌上看

——李聲振

135

Climbing Qi-Lin   扒麒麟

竹枝詞

祝罷慈雲禮善才
衣香人影上蓬萊
兒家自了燒香願
爲乞麒麟特地來

——蔡士堯

* 民間習俗，認爲麒麟是能送子的瑞獸，故市井多有舞弄麒麟的雜耍。
* Qi-lin: the unicorn, a Chinese mythic animal of deer type.

十
九
世
紀
中
國
市
井
風
情

136

劁雞佬   A Man Castrating Chicken

63

鎅木   Cutting Wood

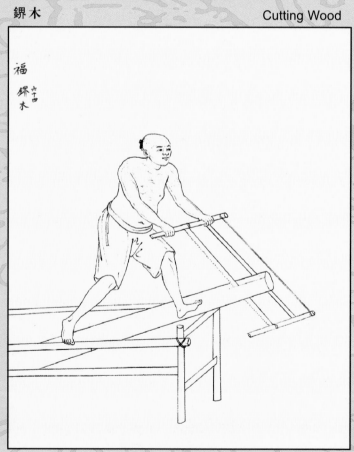

＊鎅，廣州方言用字，讀若 gai，意爲裁割。

三百六十行 360 PROFESSION

Painting Porcelain   寫瓷器

福

六十五

寫磁器

65

竹枝詞

水光山色座中招
瓷器精工用淡描
茶葉多兼瓜子大
沿河館比後湖高

——劉士璋

* 瓷，原作磁。

Selling Fujian Cake   賣福建糕

竹枝詞

明姜通透賽冰糖
橘餅紅酥蜜餞黃
縷切東瓜較甜味
棗糕畢竟占酸香

——杭世駿

福

六十六

賣福建糕

66

* Fujian is a province near by Canton.

十九世紀中國市井風情

138

賣煙　　　　　　　　　　　　　　　Selling Tobacco

竹枝詞

下流生意是裝煙
不論生人也拍肩
一度逢他抽兩口
每逢三節始開錢

——葉調元

補鑊　　　　　　　　Patching Cooker

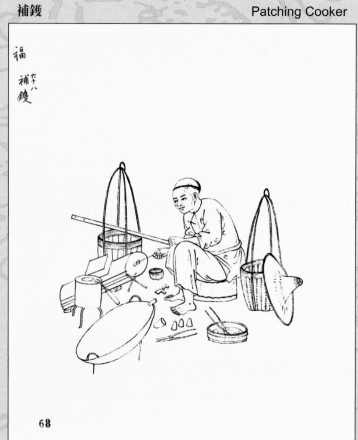

十九世紀中國市井風情

Selling Water Chestnut

賣馬蹄

竹枝詞

火藥局邊紅莧遲
恰同上市白鱗鰣
滿肩多是江鄉味
臥聽街頭賣荸薺

——翟金生

福
六十九
賣馬蹄

69

139

Dog Hulling Rice

狗舂碓

竹枝詞

雙蹄拱拜唱鳴鳴
圈套回環走自如
黃耳自饒千里健
平原誰寄一封書

——李聲振

福
狗舂碓
七十

70

* A beggar with his dog trained to hull rice for entertaining people.

十九世紀中國市井風情

140

賣假鬃   Selling False Hair

* 當是一種賣假鬃髮的行當。

整蚊煙   Making Mosquito Incense

十九世紀中國市井風情

Selling Flower　　　　　　　　　賣花

竹枝詞

聞道鵝潭有白鵝
白鵝不見見清波
花叢飛出雙蝴蝶
隨著賣花人過河

——張維屏

Soliciting for Alms　　　　　　　　化香米

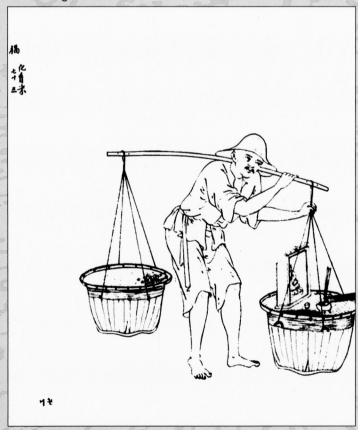

＊化，佛教用詞，化緣的化。

十九世紀中國市井風情

142

賣掃把   Selling Brooms

15

* 掃，原作蹄，據畫面改正。

賣桐油灰   Selling Tong Oil Mud

16

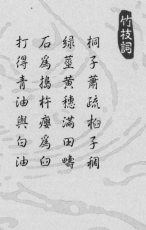

竹枝詞

桐子蕭疏栢子稠
綠莖黃穗滿田疇
石窩搗杵癭爲臼
打得青油與白油

—— 石方洛

* It is made of a kind of ashes mixed with tung oil. Tung
is a tree, its academic name is "aleurites coedata".

三百六十行 360 PROFESSION

十九世紀中國市井風情

Selling Medical Pills　　　　　　　　賣藥丸

＊ 原題如此，參見頁64。

竹枝詞

慎堂丸藥早蜚聲
老鋪街名在太平
強腎摩腰都得法
黃家還有自來精

——胡子晋

143

Selling Bamboo Baskets
and Steam Cooking Wares　　　　　賣蘿斗蒸籠

十九世紀中國市井風情

春米　　　　　　　　　Hulling rice

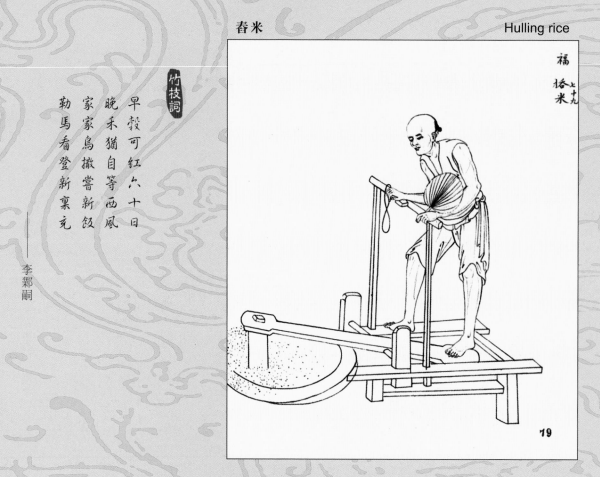

福
㫪
米

19

竹枝詞

勒馬看登新稟充
家家烏猶自等西風
晚禾猶自等西風
早穀可紅六十日

——李鄞嗣

賣魚圓　　　　　　Selling Fish Ball

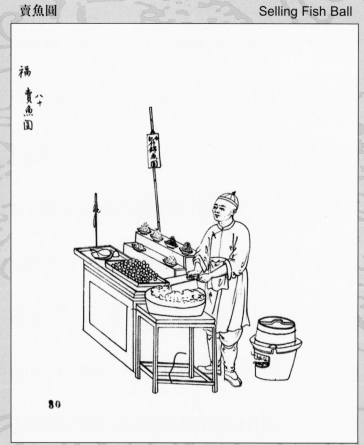

福
賣魚圓
八十

80

竹枝詞

魚餐圓子滾雞湯
切麵豆絲乾線粉
一頓狼餐飯可忘
三天過早異平常

——葉調元

* Fish ball: a food with small spherical form, made of raw fish.

三百六十行 360 PROFESSION

十九世紀中國市井風情

A Physiognomist　　　　　　　　睇相先生

竹枝詞

與君對面語平和
先問年庚是幾何
談相全憑青白眼
評量真喜閱人多

——李靜山

A Visiting Physician　　　　　　　　訪醫先生

竹枝詞

燒丹方士羽衣翩
南漢君王冀永年
指點藥洲空瓦礫
何曾天下有神仙

——江仲瑜

十九世紀中國市井風情

146

擂鼓　　　　　　　　　　　Beating Drum

竹枝詞

魚鱗古瓦覆僧寮
鐘鼓聲中自暮朝
花塔如新光塔舊
兩支文筆插青宵

——江仲瑜

賣月餅　　　　　　　　　　Selling Moon Cake

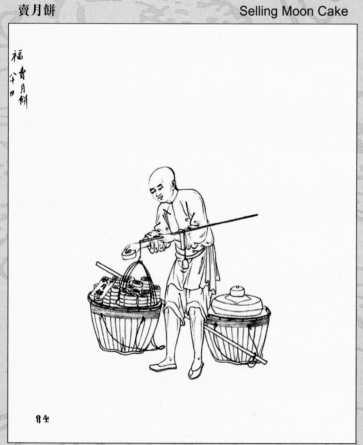

竹枝詞

中秋賞月競開筵
月餅堆盤月樣圓
禮斗香還燒大斗
南園向最盛香煙

——秦榮光

三百六十行 360 PROFESSION

Selling Melons 　　　　　　　　　　　　　賣瓜

福
賣瓜
八十五

85

竹枝詞

出入玄關詫妙詮
賣瓜不記種瓜年
王婆去後無消息
孤負橋頭月影圓

——吳濂

Twisting Silk 　　　　　　　　　　　　　絞絲

竹枝詞

五色絲繅織錦衾
織成紅綠淺和深
怪他不識鴛鴦錦
但織回紋寄妾心

——郭鍾岳

福
八十六
絞絲

86

* 絞，原作角，音近而俗借。

十
九
世
紀
中
國
市
井
風
情

148

繡錦　　　　　　　　　　　　　Embroidering Stain

竹枝詞

海珠寺前江水奔
諸洋作舶如雲屯
十三行裏居奇貨
刺繡何如倚市門

———
鮑鉁

賣涼粉　　　　　　　　　　　　Selling Cold Jelly

竹枝詞

豆花涼粉妙調和
日日擔從市上過
生小女兒偏嗜辣
紅油滿碗不嫌多

———
邢棻

三百六十行 360 PROFESSIONS

十九世紀中國市井風情

Selling Clothing Bamboo　　　賣衣裳竹

福
賣衣裳竹
八十九

89

* The bamboo stick is for hanging cloths for drying.

Selling Newspaper　　　賣新文

竹枝詞

一紙新聞海上傳
旁搜博采廣敷宣
所聞所見末聞見
拉雜書成日日編

———陳坤

福
賣新文
九十

90

* 新文可能是當時對 newspaper 的譯詞，後譯作新聞。

十九世紀中國市井風情

150

賣蒲團　　　　　　　　　　　Selling Round Cushion

竹枝詞

個個蒲團一串珠
阿彌陀佛念南無
念聲漸歇緣何事
探听風情說小姑

——童謙孟

賣豉油　　　　　　　　　　Selling Soy Oil

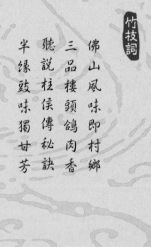

竹枝詞

佛山風味即村鄉
三品樓頭鴿肉香
聽說柱侯傳秘訣
半緣豉味獨甘芳

——胡子晉

三百六十行 360 PROFESSION

Sealing Bullion　　　　　　　　　　封元寶

福
九十三
封元寶

93

竹枝詞

白雲山上白雲籠
古冢白楊雨氣蒙
三月踏青人上墓
紙錢麥飯繞東風

——單璞石

* 賣一種紙做的金銀元寶，用以作爲祭品。

* Selling a kind of bullion made of paper, it is used in sacrifice for some one can use it in the other world.

Purchasing Silver Tails　　　　　　收買銀尾

福
九十四
收買銀尾

竹枝詞

買賣空頭入市忙
友分好淡幻黃粱
幾多勝敗如輪轉
權把銀場作戰場

——胡子晉

94

* 銀尾，是銀兩反復流通後剩餘的碎銀。

* Silver Tails are the scrappy silver. The silver is cut again and again in its circulating course, after then its small remainders need be collected and smelted once again.

十九世紀中國市井風情

車煙桿　　　　　　　　　　　　　　Making Tobacco Pipe

福
車煙
竿
九十五

95

燒瓷器　　　　　　　　　　　　　　Burning China Ware

福
燒磁
器
九十六

96

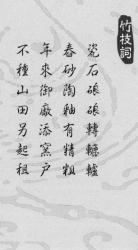

竹枝詞

瓷石磠磠轉轆轤
舂砂陶釉有精粗
年來御廠添窯戶
不種山田另起租

——查慎行

三百六十行 360 PROFESSIONS

十九世紀中國市井風情

A Man Hunting Bird　　　　打雀佬

福
打雀佬
九十七

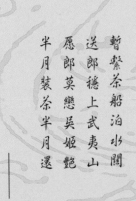

97

竹枝詞

斑魚黃雀盡充廚
風味由來數夏湖
市遠不妨留客醉
茅柴新釀貫村壚

——朱麟應

Shouldering Tea　　　　擔茶

竹枝詞

暫繫茶船泊水關
送郎穩上武夷山
願郎莫戀吳姬艷
半月裝茶半月還

——陳冕英

福
擔茶
九十八

98

賣關刀　　　　　　　　Selling Guan's Sword

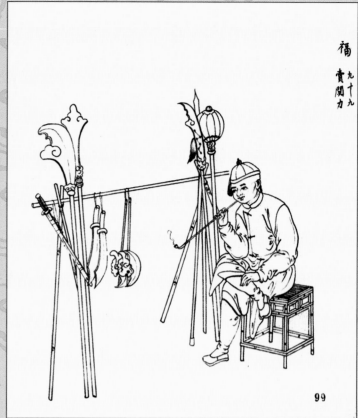

99

竹枝詞

大洲男兒身姓熊
把頭削鐵刃如風
直前竟斬紅旗首
步戰須還第一功

——周霆震

* 關刀，關公的刀，實際上是玩具武器的代稱。
* Guan's sword, Guan Gong's sword, exactly
  is a general term for toy weapons.

蒸酒　　　　　　　　　Distilling Liquor

100

竹枝詞

一望黃雲被繡塍
如墉如櫛慶三登
勸郎多種羊脂糯
十月新篘勝紹興

——孫圃

154

十九世紀中國市井風情

Selling Pork 　　　　賣豬肉

竹枝詞

十日黃雞五日豬
大家入市趁朝圩
惠州飽飫東坡飯
風景難忘是故居

——趙希璜

101

155

Making Shoes 　　　　做靴

竹枝詞

蠻靴精緻出心裁
五色斑斕錦繡堆
最是月明人靜後
惝聲閣閣踏霜來

——孫兆溎

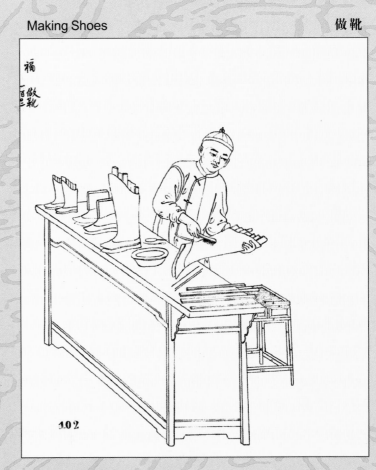

102

十九世紀中國市井風情

塗沙佬　　　　　　　　　　　　　　A Man Panning Sand

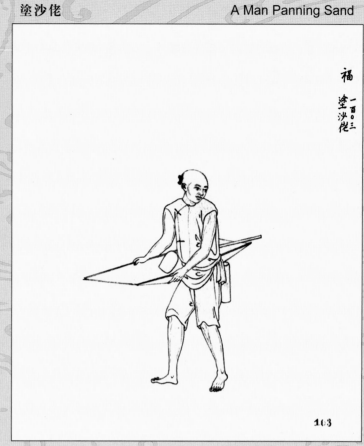

福
一百〇三
塗沙佬

103

* 塗，疑當作淘，音近而訛。

補遮　　　　　An Umbrella Repairman

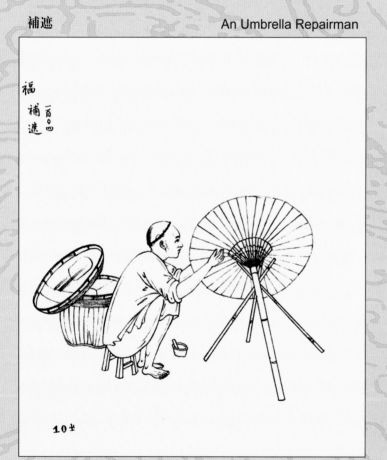

福
補遮
一百〇四

104

* 廣州方言，傘作遮。

竹枝詞

輕移蓮步影徘徊
華蓋雲呈五色開
要使清風無可染
元規塵闘拂人來

——陳坤

Chiseling Design on Locks　　　　　鑿鎖花

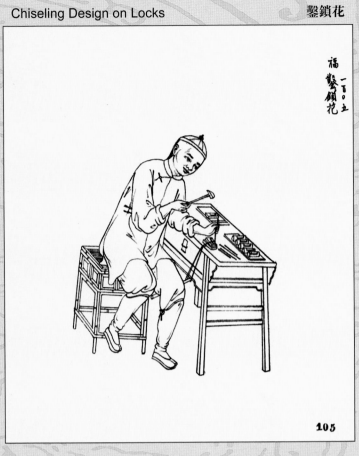

福
鑿鎖花
一百〇五

105

Painting Flower on Jade　　　　　點翠花

福
点翠花
一百〇六

106

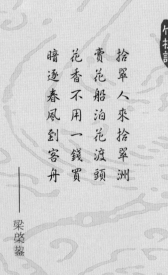

竹枝詞

拾翠人來拾翠洲
賣花船泊泊花渡頭
花香不用一錢買
暗逐春風到客舟

——梁槤鉹

十九世紀中國市井風情

158

賭糖膠　　　　　　　　　　　　　Cleaning Tang-Jiao

107

＊ 此圖原題如此，似有誤。參見頁 42。

賣眼鏡　　　　　　　　　　Selling Spectacles

108

竹枝詞

車從熱鬧道中行
斜坐觀書不出聲
眼鏡戴來裝近視
學他名士老先生

——楊米人

十九世紀中國市井風情

Selling Medical Plaster 賣膏藥

竹枝詞

南州水土感炎蒸
患伏深時疾易乘
誤煞庸醫多不解
分明疗毒作癍稱

——陳坤

109

Packaging 打包

竹枝詞

長壽門前列百塵
謀生偶合有前緣
無多傭值還多事
辛苦年年作往年

——陳坤

110

十九世紀中國市井風情

160

擔魚種　　　　　Transporting Fish Fry

福
一百十一
擔魚種

111

竹枝詞

才有魚苗更值錢
尋常一樣湘南水
漁家生計大江邊
春雨春雷欲曉天

——黃家驥

打更　　　　A Night Watchman

福
二百十二
打更

112

竹枝詞

一天雨後便成溝
只恐低窪難泄水
氣象居然百里侯
官衙小小有更樓

——高小雲

Polishing Tin Ware   磨錫器

竹枝詞

湘子橋頭夜色清
上元燈火接春城
揭陽美錫潮陽匠
裝遍長簪又短簪

——陶元藻

A Visiting Physician for All Diseases   訪醫雜症

竹枝詞

九家巫覡一家醫
起死還憑視鬼師
莫忘歲時勤拜禱
八鼇酒酹七姑祠

——陳文瑞

賣鹹菜　　　　　　　　　　Selling Salty Vegetable

竹枝詞

菜味冬來越覺甜
新薑冷脆把鹽醃
冰壺醒酒嚴寒夜
墻角親懸雪甕籤

—— 秦榮光

115

賣天窗　　　　　　　　Selling Sky Window

竹枝詞

窗嵌明瓦比玻璃
才蔽驕陽日又西
一樣玲瓏難透影
不教花月怨迷離

—— 陳坤

116

* Sky window, translucent roof.

三百六十行 360 PROFESSIONS

162

A Purchasing Agent　　　　　　　　　　賣辦

竹枝詞

要知貴賤有來因
秤手虛抬莫認真
信口喝錢斜眼視
還分面熟面生人

——童謙孟

* 此時賣辦有采辦的意思。

Selling Calligraphy and Painting　　　　賣字畫

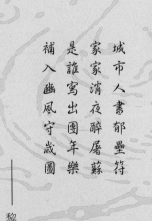

竹枝詞

城市人書郁墨符
家家消夜醉屠蘇
是誰寫出團年樂
補入豳風守歲圖

——黎箕垣

十九世紀中國市井風情

164

鑿磨　　　　　　　　　　　　　　　　　Making Millstone

剃頭仔　　　　　　　　　　　A Barber

竹枝詞

肩隨擔具剃頭來
此是旗人首創開
市上至今猶不少
無資設店籍圖財

——佚名

十九世紀中國市井風情

A Calligrapher　　　　　　　　寫大字

竹枝詞

室中點綴不容慳
仲約聯屏亦等閒
聞說更生太高價
近來寫字好蕭嫻

——胡子晉

165

A Bow and Arrow Maker　　　　　整弓箭

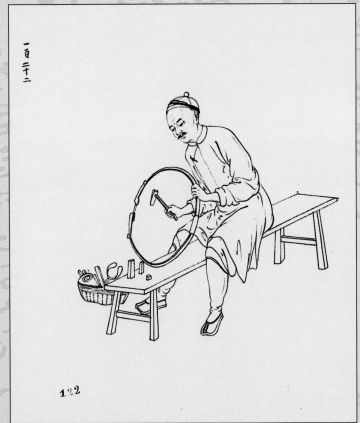

* 標題原缺，今據畫面補。
* No title on original picture, it is added in
  accordance with the painting's appearance.

三百六十行 360 PROFESSIONS

十九世紀中國市井風情

166

賣蚊煙　　　　　　　　Selling Mosquito Incense

賣火腿　　　　　　　　Selling Ham

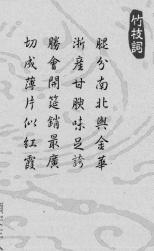

腿分南北與金華
浙產甘腴味足誇
勝會開筵銷最廣
切成薄片似紅霞

——頤安主人

十九世紀中國市井風情

Selling Black Olives　　　　　　　　　　賣杬豉

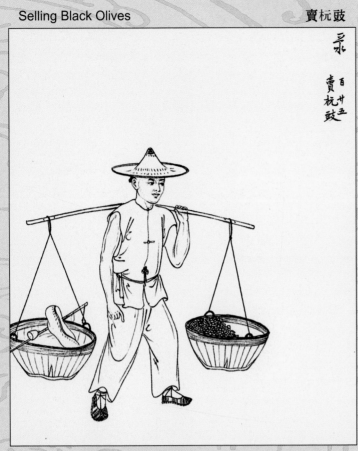

近從莞順遠雷廉
海舶年年歲月淹
白䖠紅蝦烏欖豉
生來不食廣州鹽

——黄笏廷

＊橄欖製的一種調味品，亦稱杬角。

167

Selling Toads　　　　　　　　　　賣蟾蜍

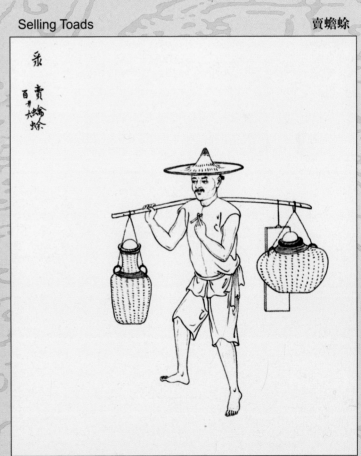

＊蟾，原作蟾，粵語俗字。

塗蜆　　　　　　　　　　　　　Catching Clams

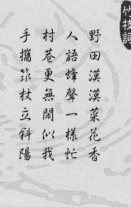

竹枝詞

蜆埠年來價漸高
蛋船終日尚勞勞
東南水利皆成稅
何地還堪漫下篙

——勞孝真

168

＊塗，疑當作淘，音近而訛。

賣枵杖　　　　　　　　Selling "Xiao" Cane

竹枝詞

野田漠漠菜花香
人語蜂聲一樣忙
村巷更無閒似我
手攜筇杖立斜陽

——朱若東

＊枵杖，空心杖、老人杖。

＊ "Xiao" cane, the cane for old people.

十九世紀中國市井風情

Cooking Clams

校蜆

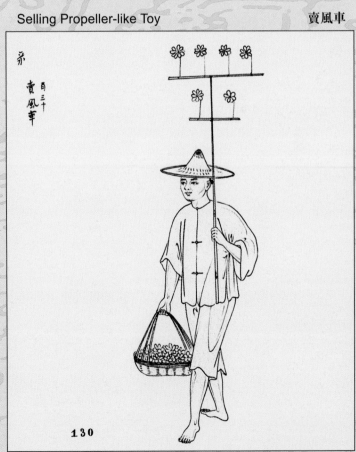

竹枝詞

春風又見送年來
太息痴人喚不回
聽取聲聲發財蜆
分明蘊利是身災

——陳坤

Selling Propeller-like Toy

賣風車

竹枝詞

端憑輪轉響丁東
豈是驅車可御風
工藝漫矜機械化
此中推動理相通

——朱醉雲

十九世紀中國市井風情

170

補衣服婆　　　　　　　　　　A Woman Patching Cloth

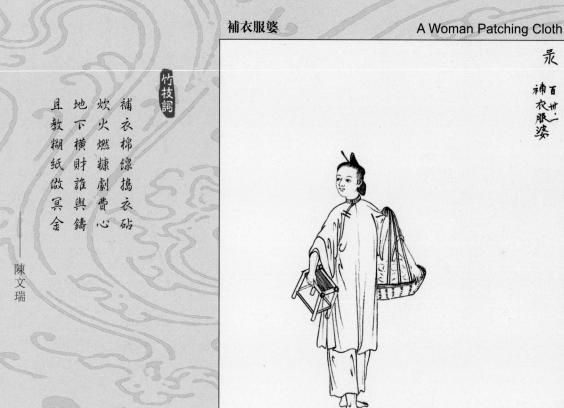

竹枝詞

補衣棉線搗衣砧
炊火燃糠劇費心
地下橫財誰與鑄
且教糊紙做冥金

——陳文瑞

擔煤炭　　　　　　　　　　Carrying Coal or Charcoal

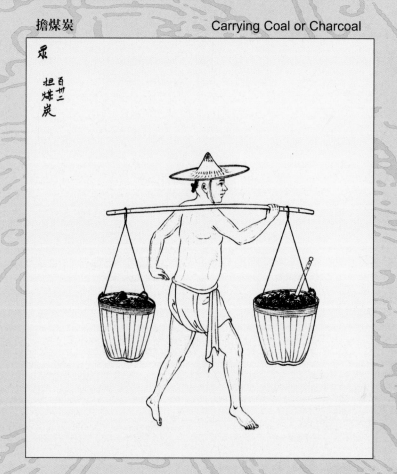

竹枝詞

華堂開處鬧新年
姊按笙簫妹譜弦
小婢好燃歡喜炭
笑花飛上鬢雲邊

——鄭瓊章

十九世紀中國市井風情

A Nun Soliciting Rice　　　師姑化米

竹枝詞

紫竹庵中擬拾身
萬千煙戶盡捐銀
紅簽粉壁粘多少
名氏親書善女人

——鄭瓊章

录
師姑化米
百廿三

171

Selling Tang Yuan　　　賣湯丸

竹枝詞

幾人能嚼菜根香
賴有元宵任爾嘗
君采晚菘儂早韭
園丁休要密闌防

——陳鍾海

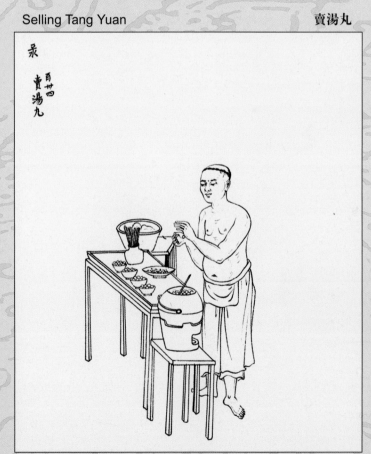

录
賣湯丸
百廿四

* Tang Yuan, a kind of desserts made of sticky rice flour
with some fillings.

十九世紀中國市井風情

賣蝦醬　Selling Shrimp Paste

竹枝詞

小甕黃虀送草南
換來佳味看來饞
一瓶蟹甲純黃醬
千箸魚頭細海鹹

——李鄴嗣

賣竹椅　Selling Bamboo Chair

竹枝詞

竹器精工勝棘猴
剝青刨白黃雕鏤
應家幾代傳孫子
秘法單方不可求

——謝階樹

三百六十行 360 PROFESSION

十九世紀中國市井風情

Selling Litchi   賣荔枝

竹枝詞

荔枝灣里荔枝香
名不虛傳十八娘
一日飽餐三百顆
教人渴想往來忙

——陳坤

173

Selling Horse Meat   賣馬肉

竹枝詞

北風雨雪門不開
景小暫作金粟堆
黃竹歌停八駿杳
一馬鳴訴悲風哀

——黃遵憲

138

十九世紀中國市井風情

賣竹枕　　　　　　　　　　Selling Bamboo Pillow

竹枝詞

龍鬚席子琉璃枕
涼月窺人人未寢
瑣瑣紗廚茉莉風
香浸玉臂羅衣冷

——曾懿

賣竹燈臺薑磨　　　Selling Bamboo Lampstand

* 薑，原作羌，因音近而俗借。

三百六十行 360 PROFESSION

十九世紀中國市井風情

Raising Pig

養豬

录

百四一

養豬

A Monkey Trainer

舞馬騮

* 標題原缺，今據畫面與頁56補。馬騮，廣州方言，讀若 ma-lau，即猴。

* No Chinese title on original picture, it is added in accordance
  with the painting's appearance and Puqua's
  painting P. 56.

十九世紀中國市井風情

箍補佬　　　　　　　　　　　　　A Cooper

托杉　　　　　　　　　　Carrying Fir

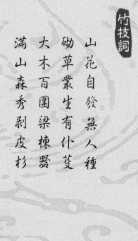

竹枝詞

山花自發無人種
砌草叢生有什葰
大木百圍梁棟器
滿山森秀剝皮杉

——謝階樹

十九世紀中國市井風情

Soliciting Money and Rice

化錢米

录
百四士
化錢米

竹枝詞

各家布施斗和升
化米都將臘八稱
饒鼓喧闐人絡繹
一群道士一群僧

——葉調元

Selling Pig-blood

賣豬血

竹枝詞

芝麻饊子叫淒涼
巷口鳴鑼賣小糖
水餃湯圓豬血擔
夜深還有滿街梆

——葉調元

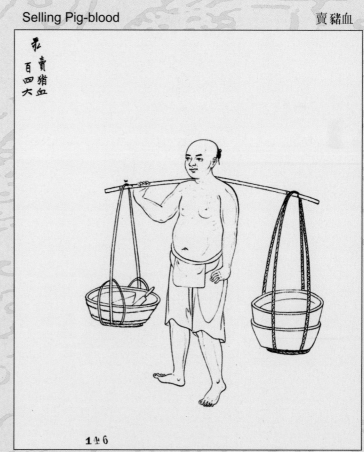

录
賣豬血
百四六

十九世紀中國市井風情

178

鑲籮　　　　Repairing Bamboo Basket

竹枝詞

花奴花叟各奔波
齊集花墟攬過河
誇郭橐駝生計活
編籮不費本錢多

——潘有爲

賣木魚書　　Selling a Kind of Popular Song Book

竹枝詞

三河港口小船樁
一半貲來是斷塘
五月十三關帝殿
唱書因爲入同行

——童謙孟

* 木魚書，一種民間唱本。

Selling Gold Fish　　　　　　　　　賣金魚

采
百四九
賣金魚

Treading Distilled Grains Cakes　　　踏酒餅

竹枝詞

不愁瘴霧與蠻煙
好趁初晴出拜年
正月家家都有酒
銀幡斜墮醉新箆

——

龔澄軒

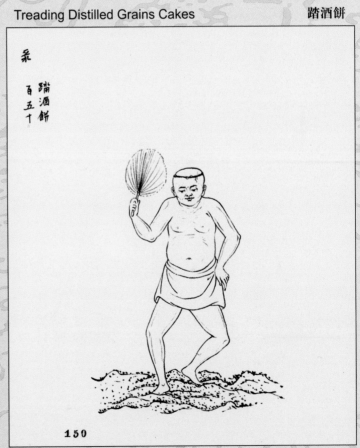

采
百五十
踏酒餅

150

* 踏，原作蹻，顯訛。

十九世紀中國市井風情

賣綠豆粥　　　　　　　Selling Mung Bean Gruel

耀米佬　　　　　A Rice Peddler

穀貴傷民賤害農
閭閻無處得從容
賣絲糴穀供官課
剜肉送瘡怕歲凶

——焦和生

三百六十行 360 PROFESSIONS

十九世紀中國市井風情

Selling Narcissus　　　　　　賣水仙花

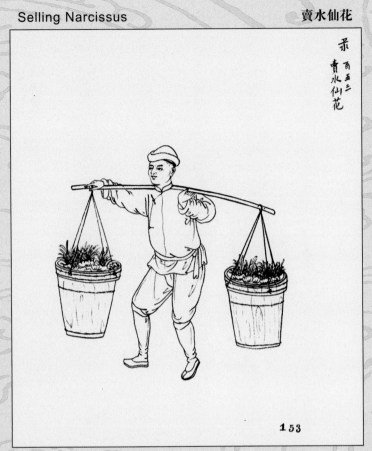

竹枝詞

宜春帖子燦云霞
爆竹聲喧鬧歲華
偏是熱場翻似淡
家家盤供水仙花

——雪裏芭蕉館

153

A Lantern Bearer in Wedding Parade　　　　親家郎

竹枝詞

三朝親戚探新娘
去去擔茶遣婢忙
線絡挑來紅捧合
煎堆斗大好油香

——陳坤

154

三百六十行 360 PROFESSIONS

十九世紀中國市井風情

擔溝渠水　　　　　　　　Carrying Ditch Water

竹枝詞

下路人家屋緊排
生人到此向難猜
佃隨水桶空挑者
直到河邊是正街

——葉調元

155

* 溝，原作鑄，訛。

刬布　　　　　　Calendering Cloth

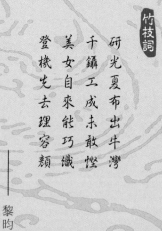

竹枝詞

研光夏布出牛灣
千鑷工成未敢悭
美女自來能巧織
登機先去理容顏

——黎昀

156

* 刬，廣州當地俗字，讀若 xin（去聲）。刬布，意爲踩滾石緊布。
* A cylinder stone was used for calendering cloth at that
time in China, just like this picture shows.

十九世紀中國市井風情

A Man both are Plasterer and Carpenter 泥木佬

录
百
五
七
坭
木
佬

157

* 泥，原作坭，俗字

Sharpening Knife 鏟刀

录
百
五
六
鏟
刀

158

三百六十行 360 PROFESSIONS

十九世紀中國市井風情

184

賣豆腐乾　　　　　　　　Selling Bean Curd Cake

竹枝詞

鄭仙昨日進神香
水汲葫蘆滌不祥
香欖松貓乾豆腐
白雲風物贈街坊

——林錄鑒

百五十九
賣豆腐肝

159

* 乾，原作肝，顯誤。

賣叮噹　　　　　　　　Selling Ding-Dang

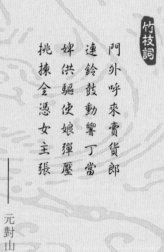

賣叮噹
百六十

160

竹枝詞

門外呼來賣貨郎
連鈴鼓動響丁當
婢供驅使娘彈壓
挑揀全憑女主張

——元對山人

* 據圖，叮噹是一種手搖鈴。

* Ding–Dang, a kind of hand bell.

Pasting Newspaper 貼新文紙

161

* 新文，即新聞，參見頁149注文。

竹枝詞

帽儿順手搶紛紛
新跌行情客未聞
幾日牛莊船不到
豆油看漲二三分

——袁翔甫

Delivering Cooking Oil 送油

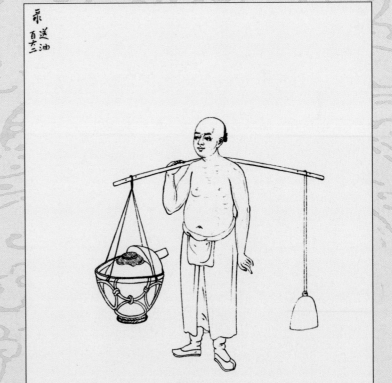

162

十九世紀中國市井風情

扱魚　　　　　　　　　　　　　　　　Fishing with a Fishing Net

竹枝詞

雁翅城邊七里通
荔枝灣裏荔枝紅
五月打鰳漁艇過
腥風陣陣逐香風

——單荔南

賣元寶　　　　　　　　　　　Selling Bullion

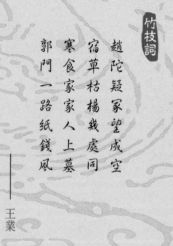

竹枝詞

趙陀疑冢望成空
宿草枯楊幾處同
寒食家家人上墓
郭門一路紙錢風

——王業

* 供祭祀用的紙元寶。

* The bullion made of paper uses for sacrifice.

三百六十行 360 PROFESSIONS

Selling Hand Warmer 賣火通

165

* 火通，小炭炉，作烘手和引燃柴火用。

* Hand warmer: a small charcoal stove.

Carrying Rice 托米

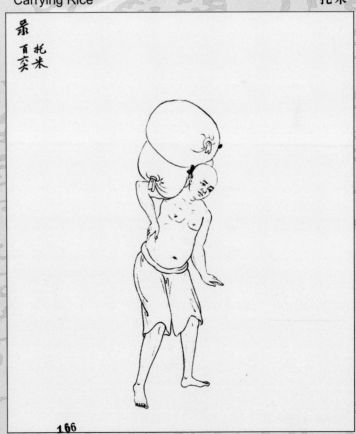

166

十九世紀中國市井風情

187

十九世紀中國市井風情

188

賣雨帽　　　　　　　　　Selling Rain Hat

167

竹枝詞

草笠芒鞋一酒壺
晚圩濃索打魚租
鄰村老叟忽逢語
問道分龍雨有無

——胡曦

賃書　　　　　　　　　Renting books

168

竹枝詞

頻摩腹笥計空疏
樂境方知是讀書
尤惜一冬閒裏過
相期志學在三餘

——陳坤

十九世紀中國市井風情

Selling Pomelos

賣桑麻柚

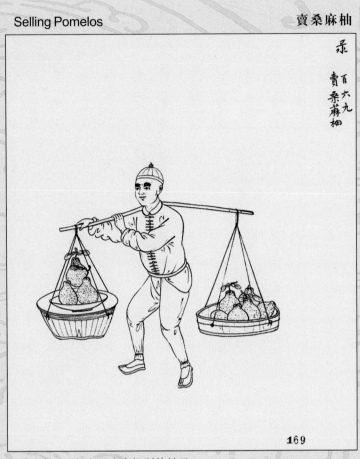

竹枝詞

黃皮柚子賤如泥
爭賞中秋月底攜
青粉墙粘紙番塔
笑他兒女鬥糖雞

——潘兆鏗

169

* 桑麻柚，一種産于廣東梅縣的柚子。

189

Making Ceremonial Visit at Relative's Tomb

拜山

竹枝詞

寒食家家掃墓還
相逢同過伏龍岡
空山日落晚風起
飛挂綫錢多白楊

——陳作舟

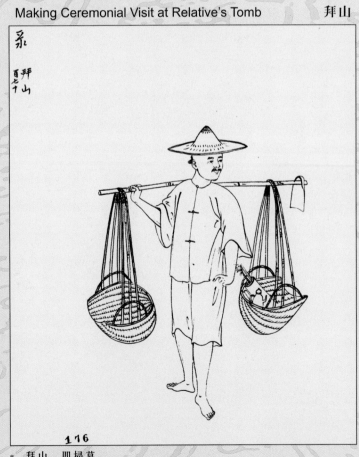

116

* 拜山，即掃墓。

十九世紀中國市井風情

190

賣罩籬   Selling Zhao-li

* Zhao-li: an implement made of thin bamboo
strips, using for covering food, and so on.

賣片糖

Selling sheet Candy

竹枝詞

糖霜和粉拌玫瑰
纖手揉成油角來
朱盒描金紅絡索
餽年呼婢送煎堆

——蜀江樵客

十九世紀中國市井風情

A Man Carrying Fire Wood　　　　　擔柴佬

录
百七三
坦柴佬

173

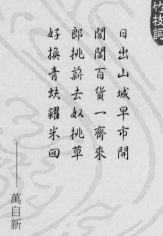

竹枝詞

日出山城早市開
閭閻百貨一齊來
郎挑薪去奴挑草
好換青蚨糴米回

——萬自新

191

A Woman Washing Cloth　　　　　洗衫婆

录
洗衫婆
百七四

114

十九世紀中國市井風情

192

織鴨籠   Weaving Duck Cage

錄百七五
織鴨籠

115

* The duck cage is made of bamboo strips.

收買佬   A Man Buying Old Articles

收買佬
錄百七六

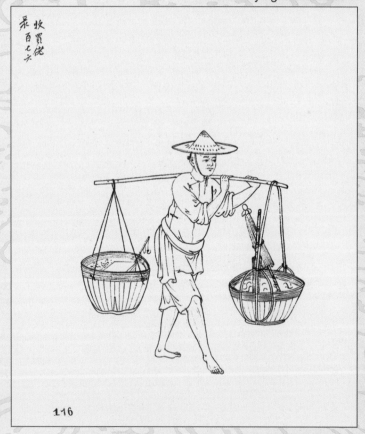

116

竹枝詞

古寺長安日出遲
鋪陳百貨欲居奇
珍奇不少傳家寶
流諸民間價不知

——葉庭勛

十九世紀中國市井風情

Selling Olives
賣白杬

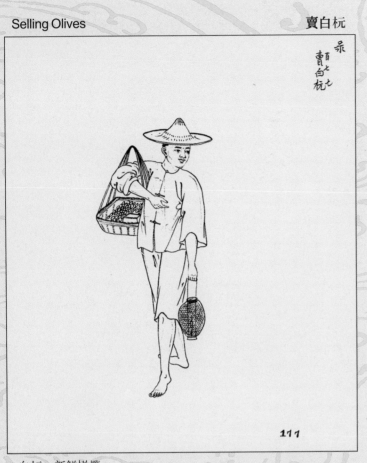

111

竹枝詞

橄欖青青滿把鮮
檳榔簍葉動相牽
何如儂縛新龍眼
一束勻圓抵一錢

——杭世駿

* 白杬，新鮮橄欖。

竹枝詞

狀猶曾無世業農
農功一半屬人傭
最憐箕內升斗米
不是農家手自舂

——童謙孟

Beating Harvest Rice
打穀

118

十九世紀中國市井風情

194

鏟茯片   Cutting Fu-ling Flakes

竹枝詞

絳跗閣前剡龍松
絳跗居士玉雪容
百餘年來猶說項
茯苓根下苔花濃

——張燕昌

179

* 鏟，原作剗，異體字；茯，茯苓的簡稱。

補鞋   A Cobbler   * Fu-ling: poris cocos.

180

Making Jewelry

打首飾

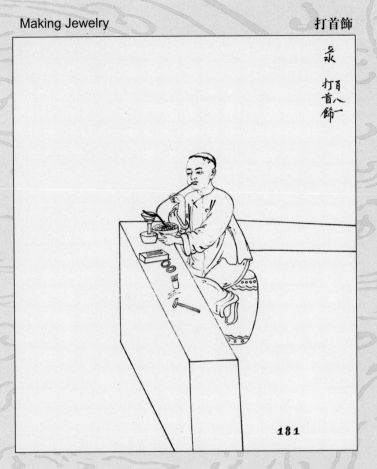

竹枝詞

妝束趨時出大家
長裙短襖小皮靴
銷魂最是風兜鬢
斜插金簪押緻花

——鈴伯

A Blind Beggar

盲乞兒

十九世紀中國市井風情

196

巡城佬

Peddling Around City

133

* 按圖，似是一環城巡走的叫賣者。

賣絃索

Selling String

184

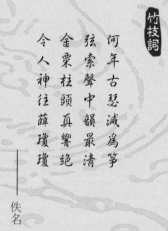

何年古瑟減爲箏
絃索聲中韻最清
金粟柱頭眞響絶
令人神往薛瓊瓊

佚名

* 絃索，此指琴弦，絃同弦。

* The string is used for instrument.

十九世紀中國市井風情

Selling Radish and Garlic　　　　賣蘿白蒜

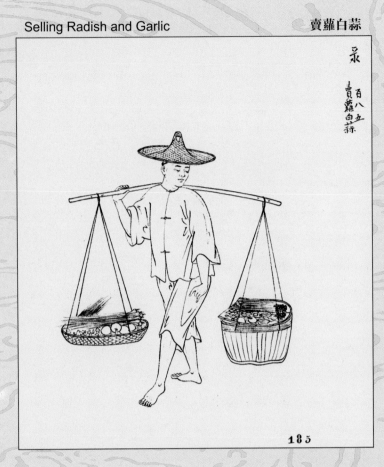

录
百八五
賣蘿白蒜

竹枝詞

三元宮畔雪盈山
都統親操總未閒
羨煞北門鄉下佬
菜蔬擔去布擔還

——萬叔子

185

A Man Turning over Nightsoil　　　　賭尿佬

竹枝詞

費收潔淨逐家催
得罪巡丁或禍胎
垃圾滿街蠅蚋惡
寄聲黃泌緩重來

——胡子晉

录
賭尿佬
百八六

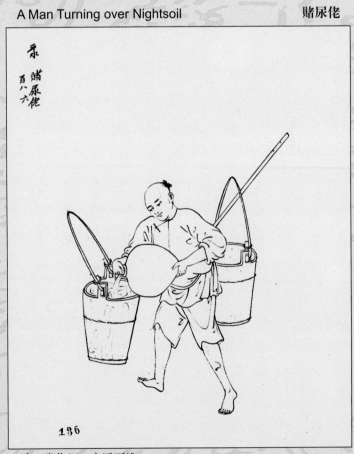

186

* 賭，當作倒，音近而訛。

十九世紀中國市井風情

竹枝詞

年年見說鬧錢荒
鑄得銀錢抵孔方
倘使盤龍輪郭好
買絲糴穀盡商量

——蔣仁

找換錢　　　　　　　Changing Money

187

賣甕缸　　　　　　Selling Large Jar

188

三百六十行 360 PROFESSIONS

Selling Paper Kite   賣紙鷂

錄
百八九
賣紙鷂

萬家秋色趙佗城
粵秀山前景物清
到處響弓齊入耳
西風吹遍紙鳶聲

——江仲瑜

189

* 鷂，原作遥，顯誤。

Match Maker   媒人公

竹枝詞

冰上人尋月裏娥
彩輿先導簫笙歌
盧茅定例錢多少
媒雄調兜合剪鵝

——胡曦

錄
九十
媒人公

190

十九世紀中國市井風情

200

賣枚馬　　　　　　　Selling Mei-ma

191

* 枚馬，一種猜數的賭博。

* Mei-ma: a gamble on guessing number.

賣頭篦　　　Selling Dense-toothed Comb

192

竹枝詞

阿母梳頭曉鏡春
東牙小巷哄街塵
攜將稀齒篦箕樣
來贈寒窗攤鬢人

——杭世駿

十九世紀中國市井風情

Selling and Delivering Vegetables　　　　賣送菜

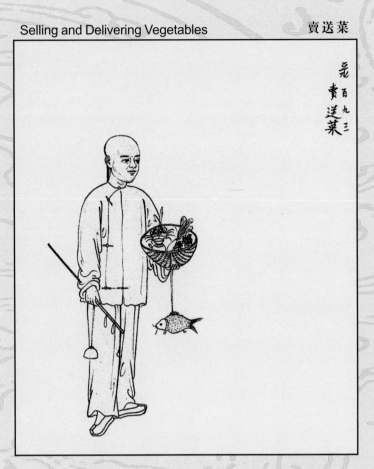

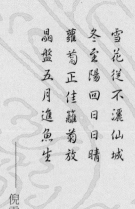

竹枝詞

雪花從不灑仙城
冬至陽回日日晴
蘿蔔正佳籬菊放
晶盤五月進魚生

——倪雲瓙

201

Selling Shoe Brush　　　　賣鞋掃

打磨 Making Stone Mill

录百九五打礶

195

* 磨，原作礶，俗字。參見頁52

奶媽送禮 A Wet Nurse Delivering Present

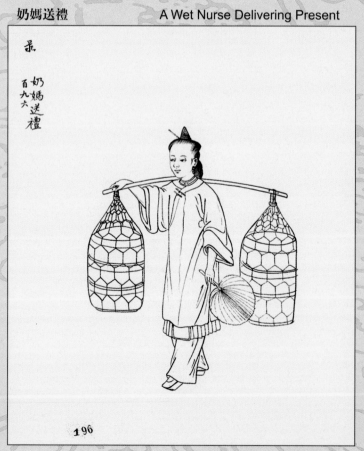

录奶媽送禮百九六

196

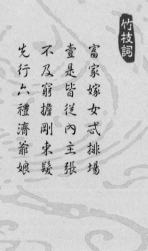

竹枝詞

富家嫁女忒排場
壹是皆從內主張
不及窮擔剛束竣
先行六禮濟爺娘

——朱文治

十九世紀中國市井風情

Carrying Baggage　　　　　　　擔鋪蓋

录百九七担擔鋪蓋

191
1

竹枝詞

雖無恒業有恒心
升斗謀為俯仰深
吃飯原非容易事
年年人海感浮沉

——陳坤

203

Collecting Dung　　　　　　　換屎精

录百九八換屎精

198

十九世紀中國市井風情

竹枝詞

得魚那可便忘筌
小市窮民不販鮮
昨日論斤街上賣
西沙新到鸕鶿船

——彭淑

教釣魚鷹　　　　　　　　　　　Training Egret

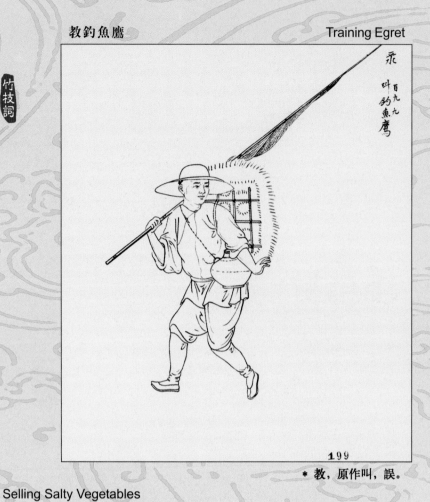

199

* 教，原作叫，誤。

賣鹹菜　　　　　Selling Salty Vegetables

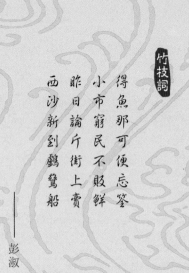

200

Winding Threads 繞綫團

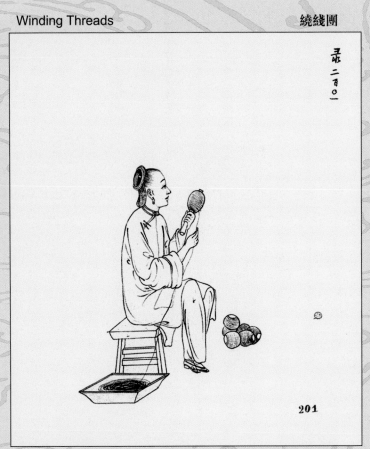

201

* 標題原缺，今據畫面補。

* No title on original picture, it is added in
  accordance with the painting's appearance.

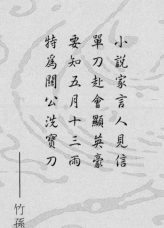

竹枝詞

特為關公洗寶刀
要知五月十三雨
單刀赴會顯英豪
小說家言人見信

——竹孫氏

Selling Guan's Sword 賣關刀

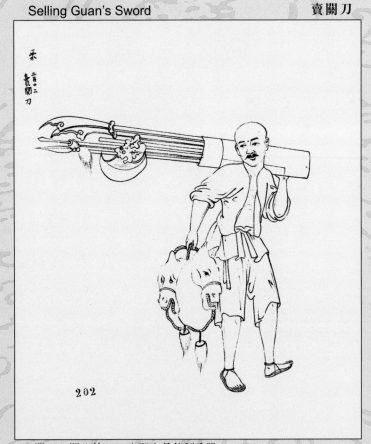

202

* 關刀，關公的刀，實際上是仿製兵器。

* Guan's sword, Guan Gong's sword, exactly is
  an imitative weapon.

十九世紀中國市井風情

賣錐　　　　　　　　　　　　　Selling Awl

A Man Panning Sand

塗沙佬

竹枝詞

北郊烽火接東郊
完卵難求懼覆巢
闔約商團齊出隊
太平橋上有沙包

——胡子晋

* 塗，疑當作淘，音近而訛。

Selling Hemp

賣麻

竹枝詞

桑麻披野綠盈盈
路靖蓬蒿戶不驚
聽水聽風都已倦
愛聽人說好收成

——王福坤

205

Playing Shuttlecock

打燕

竹枝詞

放學歸來日未曛
滾錢拋毽鬧成群
阿娘膝下頻需索
吹了糖人捏面人

——葉調元

206

＊打燕，即踢毽子。

十九世紀中國市井風情

賣武　Demonstrating Gong-fu for Living

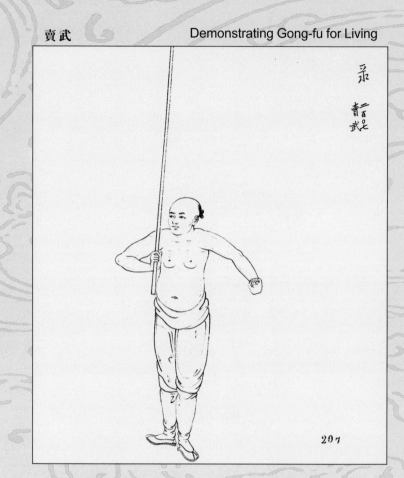

竹枝詞

少年都曉易筋經
拔距翹關事事能
飽我老拳遺毒手
吾師不讓少林僧

——謝階樹

賣蕃薯　Selling Sweet Potato

竹枝詞

夏至今無西北風
瓜蔬果腹不嫌豐
菜鮮人嗜潮州白
薯美濃食北地紅

——佚名

* 北地紅薯，俗呼爲蕃薯。

三百六十行 360 PROFESSION

Writing Spring Festival Scrolls 寫輝春

竹枝詞

銅壺滴滴夜無聲
爆竹如雷響滿城
貼罷宜春人小醉
看花听唱到天明

——倪雲癯

209

* 輝春，即春聯之類。

A Geomancer Examining Site of Building or Grave 睇風水

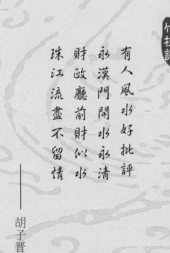

竹枝詞

有人風水好批評
永漢門開水永清
財政廳前財似水
珠江流盡不留情

——胡子晉

* 睇，即看。

十九世紀中國市井風情

賣火筒　　　　　　　　　　　　　　　　Selling Fire Pipe

* 火筒，以竹段做成，中掏空，一端竹節留下圓面鑿一小孔，燒竈時用以吹氣通火。
* This pipe is made of a part of thicker bamboo, uses for firing in the stove.

211

210

賣芋頭　　　　　　　　　　　　　　Selling Taro

212

竹枝詞

年終餽送尚奢華
彩盒肩挑倩小娃
新嫁娘於新手段
芋頭雕出四時花

——江仲瑜

十九世紀中國市井風情

Selling Mixed Soup　　　　　賣什錦湯

錄
二百十三
賣什錦湯

竹枝詞

珠江遺俗等荊湘
四月初開浴佛場
一樹菩提光孝寺
朱門分送五香湯

——江仲瑜

211

Grinding Sesame Oil　　　　　磨麻油

錄
二百十四
磨蔴油

竹枝詞

芝麻販運向寧寥
研得麻油內地銷
近日雜糧成鬧市
斗量車載海船漂

——羅四峰

* 磨，原作礳，異體字。

十九世紀中國市井風情

212

磨米　　　　　　　　　　　　　　Grinding Rice

竹枝詞

雜糧隨地可常栽
薯芋花生到處培
精穀易錢粗自用
田家勤苦亦堪哀

——焦和生

215

* 磨，原作礳，俗字。

賣蛇羌　　　　　　　　　　　　Selling Snake

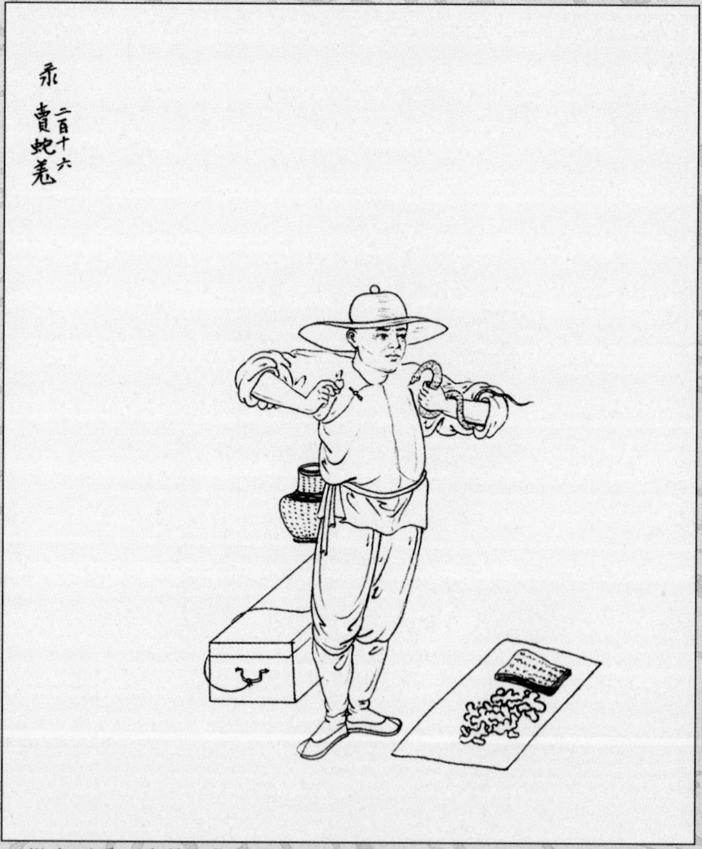

* 從畫面看，當是出售蛇產品和蛇藥。
* A man sells snake and related medicines.

十九世紀中國市井風情

Drying Lacquer 　　　　　　　　　　曬漆

* A painter lacquers a wooden board under the sun.

竹枝詞

典當生涯屬西老
籤條花工盡黃幫
江西漆鋪兼銀匠
挑水人尤霸一方

——竹孫氏

Sawing Timber 　　　　　　　　　　鋸木

竹枝詞

湖堤中段最繁沖
列市金工與木工
鋸屑霜飛撕枝料
椎聲雷震打煙筒

——葉調元

213

十九世紀中國市井風情

銼碼子　　　　　　　　　　　　　　　　Filing Weight

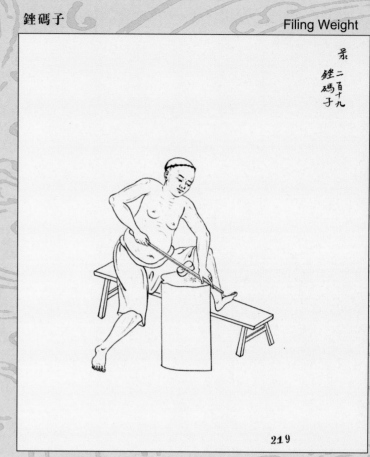

* A man files a weight to make it precise.

托貨辦　　　　　　　　　Carrying Goods

三百六十行 360 PROFESSION

十九世紀中國市井風情

Selling Melon and Vegetable　　　　　賣瓜菜

錄
二百廿
賣瓜菜

竹枝詞

一擔蔬果趁芳辰
喚醒千門萬戶人
道是當今新出個
買將多少去嘗新

——郭有光

221

Selling Stocking and Hat　　　　　賣襪帽

竹枝詞

樹裏歌聲水面腔
阿奴生小住珠江
凌波只恐塵生步
不著鴉頭襪一雙

——杭世駿

錄
二百廿二
賣襪帽

222

十九世紀中國市井風情

216

送鷄酒　　　　Delivering Chicken and Wine

* 通常是爲了婚禮。
* It is usually to a wedding family for celebration. The man who delivers a cock and a jar of wine is a coolie— serving for his master.

賣月餅　　　　Selling Moon Cake

竹枝詞

芋魁個個餅層層
慶賀中秋習俗仍
十萬人家三五夜
有樓臺處有紅燈

——倪雲臞

* The moon cakes are consumed during the Mid-autumn Festival, on the 15th of eighth lunar month.

三百六十行 360 PROFESSIONS

十九世紀中國市井風情

Selling Sword

賣劍

225

* Chinese sword with double-edged.

竹枝詞

燈火書聲古佛樓
雞靈峰頂月輪秋
昨宵有客談天象
倚劍橫空看斗牛

——胡曦

竹枝詞

機聲軋軋出柴扉
低壓蘆花見酒旗
社鼓敲殘人欲散
山翁沉醉卻忘歸

——鄧燦垣

Selling Tong-rong Flower

賣通絨花

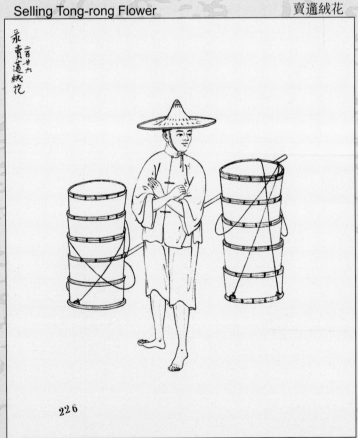

226

* 通絨花，當是用通草紙等做成的花，因通草紙極易破碎，故需用籠屜存放。
* Tong-rong Flower: A kind of artificial flower made of pith paper and others.

十九世紀中國市井風情

218

報子　　　　　　　　　　　　　　　　A Messenger

227

竹枝詞

今朝小的喝三杯
討賞門前無別話
添喜紅條便報來
高升高中�高才

——張子秋

* 報子，報告消息，特別是速報中舉的消息的人。
* The messenger announces some news, especially of passing the examination, to some one.

賣糖瓜　　　　　　　　　Selling Candy

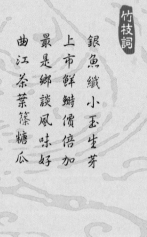

228

竹枝詞

曲江茶葉篠糖瓜
最是鄉談風味好
上市鮮鮴價倍加
銀魚纖小玉生芽

——陳文瑞

三百六十行 360 PROFESSIONS

十九世紀中國市井風情

Selling Hemp Threads and Poles

賣麻骨

录
二百廿九
賣麻骨

229

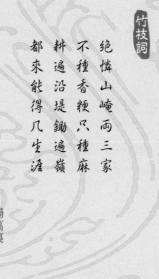

竹枝詞

絕憐山墹兩三家
不種香粳只種麻
耕遍沿堤鋤遍嶺
都來能得幾生涯

——楊萬裏

219

Selling Roast Meat

賣燒肉

录
二百三十
賣燒肉

竹枝詞

淞南叢竹密成林
屋在林中綠蔭深
入饌經年常食筍
花豬燒肉味忘心

——秦榮光

230

十九世紀中國市井風情

補花碗　　　　　　　　　　　Patching Porcelain Bowl

録補花碗　丁百卅一

231

竹枝詞

雙塔巍巍北寺前
江湖趕節鬧新年
僧房買得江西碗
五彩描來花樣鮮

——陸增

賣檳榔　　　　　　　　Selling Betel Nut

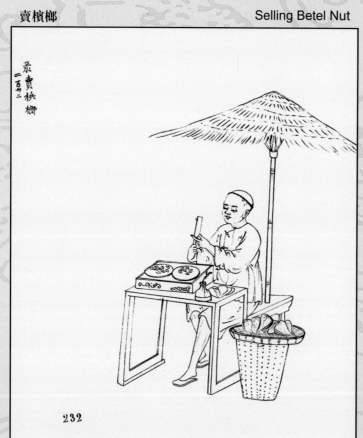

録賣檳榔　二百卅二

232

竹枝詞

種得檳榔花正香
離離多子熟檳榔
檳榔要與浮留配
咀嚼才知好味長

——陳坤

* 檳，原作桄，俗字。

十九世紀中國市井風情

Selling Wild Fox　　　　　　　　　賣野狸

233

竹枝詞

小樓秋思五羊城
藥裹茶鐺最不情
一卷吟殘花信集
木樨如霰落簾旌

——鄧方

Selling Shen-qu Tea　　　　　　賣神曲茶

234

* 神曲是一種中藥，加入此藥做成的茶餅叫神曲茶，產于福建。

* Shen-qu is a Chinese medicine. Shen-qu Tea has a round cake form, mixed Shen-qu with tea. It was produced in Fujian at that time.

三百六十行 360 PROFESSIONS

十九世紀中國市井風情

222

賣香 Selling Incense

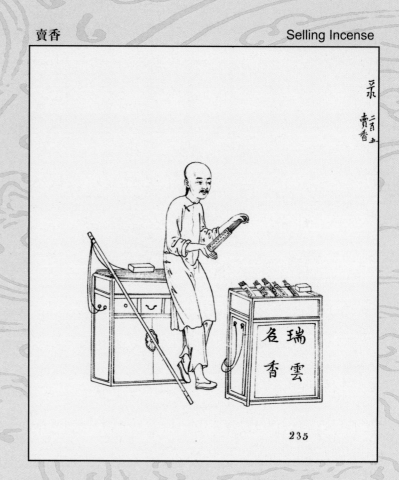

補籮斗 Repairing Bamboo Sieves

Selling Fu-Ling Cake   賣茯苓糕

录
二百卅七
賣茯苓羔

231

* 糕，原作羔，俗字。

* Fu-ling: poris cocos.

Selling Smuggled Salt   賣私鹽

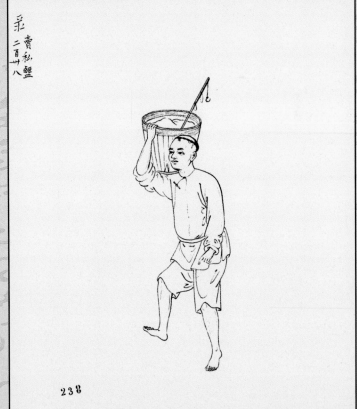

录
二百卅八
賣私鹽

238

竹枝詞

行鹽原是靠商人
其奈商人又赤貧
私賣怕官官賣絕
海邊餓肚化冤磷

——

鄭燮

十九世紀中國市井風情

便換銀　　　　　　　　　Conveniently Exchanging Silver

焙鴨蛋　　　　　　　Baking Duck Egg

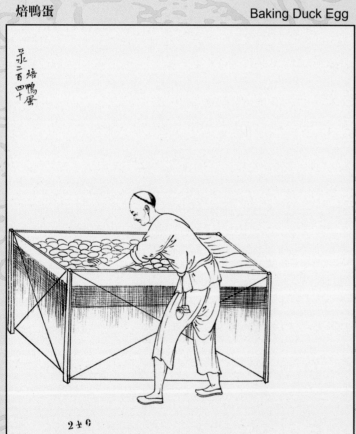

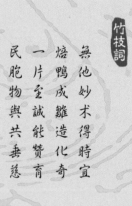

無他妙術得時宜
焙鴨成雛造化奇
一片至誠能贊育
民胞物與共垂慈

——陳坤

* 焙，人工用炭火孵化鴨蛋。

三百六十行 360 PROFESSION

十九世紀中國市井風情

Selling Water Melon　　　　　　賣西瓜

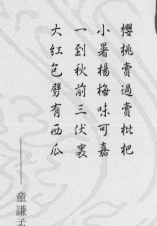

竹枝詞

櫻桃賣過賣枇杷

小暑楊梅味可嘉

一到秋前三伏裏

大紅色劈有西瓜

——童謙孟

225

Weaving and Patching Clothes　　　　織補衣服

十九世紀中國市井風情

彈棉花　　　　　　　　　Fluffing Cotton

竹枝詞

東舍新娘坐揀花
軋花媼老住西家
一弓絕妙彈花手
搓就棉條待紡紗

——秦榮光

演法　　　　Performing Tricks

竹枝詞

迎神報賽幾經秋
吐水吞刀法術優
安得西門賢太守
廓清猶弊付東流

——陳坤

三百六十行 360 PROFESSION

Selling Bean Curd　　　　　賣豆腐

竹枝詞

一年好景喜同行
唧唧喂喂訴不清
有約明朝須過我
儂家豆腐餡魚生

——王福坤

＊魚生豆腐爲供客上品。

壽
賣豆腐

三百四五

245

Playing Lian-qiang　　　　　打簾鎗

壽
打簾鎗

二百四六

246

* 簾鎗，一種竹制民間打擊樂器，中置銅錢，拍擊有聲，亦稱蓮花落。
* Lian-qiang: a kind of popular percussion instrument in China, made of thin bamboo with some copper cashes. Its another name is Lian-hua-luo.

十九世紀中國市井風情

打首飾　　　　　　　　　　　　Making Jewelry

壽
二百四七
打百飾

247

* 飾，原作餻，顯誤。

扒龍舟　　　　Playing with a Dragon Boat

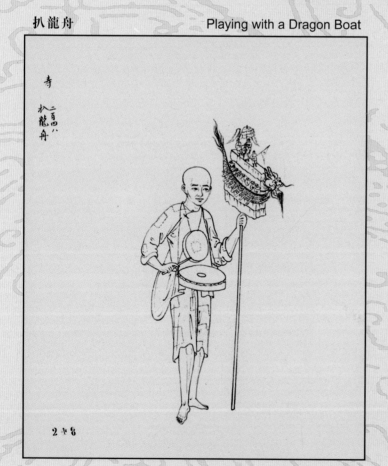

壽
二百四八
扒龍舟

248

竹枝詞

上元燈火六街紅
人影衣香處處同
一笑相逢無別訊
誰家燈虎裝來工

——陳坤

三百六十行 360 PROFESSION

十九世紀中國市井風情

229

Catching Shrimp 捉蝦

竹枝詞

水國魚蝦總等閒
朝朝入市足盤餐
兩家各飽江湖味
郎在蠔欄妾蟹欄

——江壬林堂

249

Selling Crab 賣蟹

竹枝詞

風腥蟶蛤杏初飛
雨滯梅林釣鰤歸
月桂花黃魚味美
霜寒菊圃蟹螯肥

——童謙孟

250

十九世紀中國市井風情

230

養蠶　　　　　　　　　　　Raising Silkworm

竹枝詞

姑惡飛鳴觸曉煙
紅蠶四月已三眠
白花滿把薰成露
紫葚盈筐不取錢

——朱彝尊

251

賣新文　　　　　　　　　　Selling Newspaper

252

* 新文可能是當時對 newspaper 的譯詞，後譯作新聞。參見頁149及185

Dancing with Lion　　　　　　　　　　　　舞獅

竹枝詞

兩盞球燈夜舞龍
紅腰花鼓響冬冬
憐他小婢嬌憮甚
斜倚珠帘擲賞封

——鄭瓊章

253

A Manchurian　　　　　　　　　滿洲佬

竹枝詞

宅房買賣憑中記
三二抽份跑路頻
督住搬遷挺容易
最防買主是旗人

——竹孫氏

254

* 原題洲作州。

十九世紀中國市井風情

232

奶媽　　　　　　　　　　　A Wet Nurse

奉
二百五五
奶媽

255

竹枝詞

三月游春去上香
弓鞋綏步到城隍
小姑偏作羞人態
不肯低頭禮奶娘

——陳映斗

賣手巾布　　Selling Handkerchief or Towel Cloth

奉
二百五六
賣手巾布

256

竹枝詞

三月采茶是清明
奴在房中繡手巾
兩旁繡的茶花朵
中間繡的采茶人

——彭淑

三百六十行 360 PROFESSIONS

十九世紀中國市井風情

Hammering Hat Liner 捶帽臺

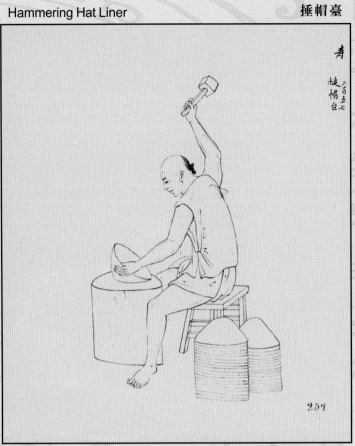

竹枝詞

第一頭顱總要尖
料應時尚鑽營計
瓜稜式樣美觀瞻
小帽新興六摺拈

——憂患生

* A man makes liners of official hats by hammering.

233

Selling Radish, Scallion and Garlic 賣蘿白葱蒜

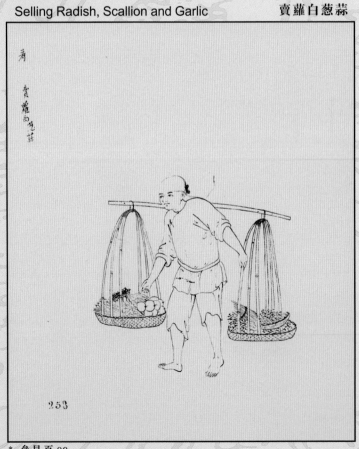

* 參見頁99。

賣鵪鶉　　　　　　　　　　　　　　　Selling Quail

竹枝詞

懸腰三兩錦囊新
入把微禽等異珍
蟋蟀者番才罷獵
又過花埭打鵪鶉

——江仲瑜

壽　賣鵪鶉　二百五九

259

賣鹹魚　　　　　　　　　　　　　　Selling Salty Fish

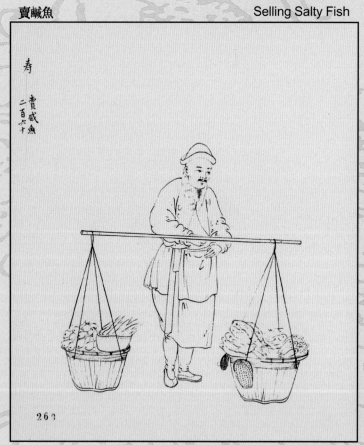

壽　賣鹹魚　二百六十

263

竹枝詞

鹹魚斟酌下晶鹽
石壓層層帶水腌
識得里湖鱗甚黑
外湖鱗白血腥粘

——郭階樹

Making Rice Cover   箍飯蓋

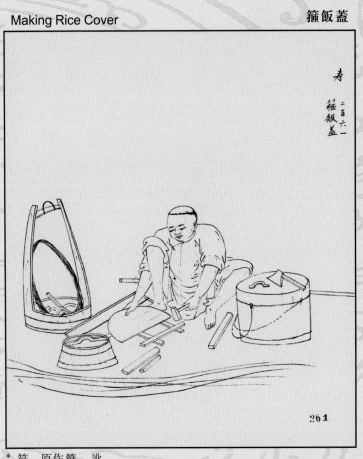

寿
二百六十一
箍飯蓋

261

* 箍，原作籮，訛。

Selling a Kind of Popular Song Book   賣木魚書

竹枝詞

琅環何必絕人間
先集一編經著錄
四庫旁羅非等閒
豐湖書藏仿焦山

——石德芬

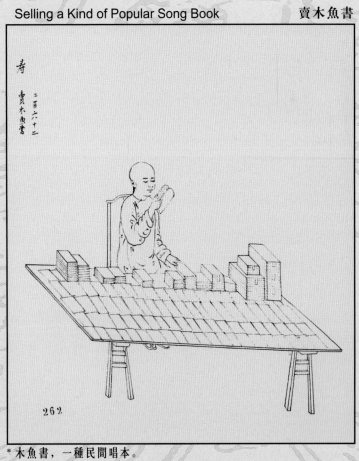

寿
二百六十二
賣木魚書

262

* 木魚書，一種民間唱本。

十九世紀中國市井風情

繡女鞋　　　　　　　Embroidering Woman's Shoe

263

竹枝詞

滿繡花鞋赤足拖
綿蠻鳥語唱新歌
靚妝倚笑偎篷坐
道是南臺科底婆

——袁綬

揸牛奶　　　　　　　Milking

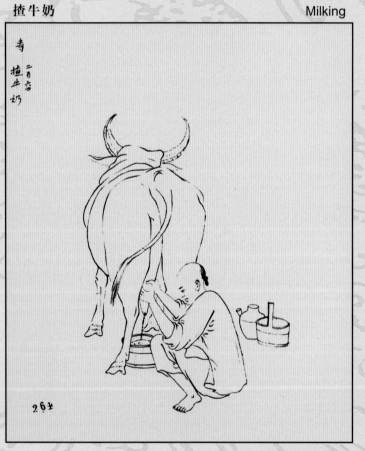

竹枝詞

晶瑩牛乳琉璃瓶
瓶口藍唇一色青
肩罅生防滋味變
芒鞋踏破露珠零

——劉景向

三百六十行 360 PROFESSIONS

十九世紀中國市井風情

Baking Pipe Stem

熨煙干

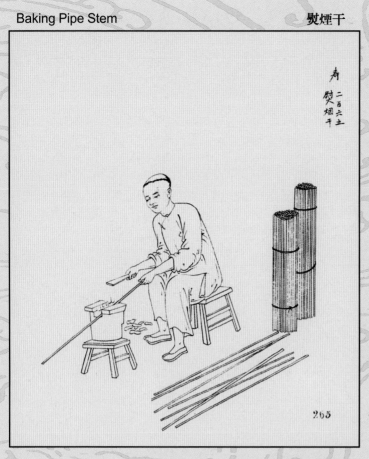

壽
二百六五
熨烟干

265

Selling Jellied Bean Curd

賣豆腐花

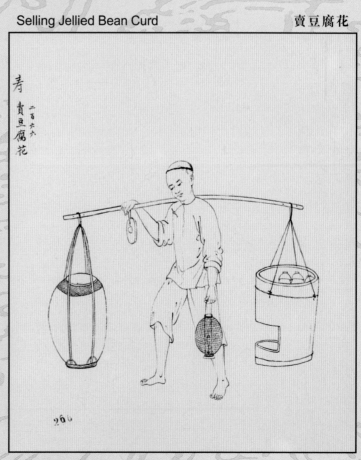

壽
賣豆腐花
二百六六

266

三百六十行 360 PROFESSIONS

十九世紀中國市井風情

238

賣薯莨　　　　　　　　　　　Selling Shu-Liang

竹枝詞

炎蒸觸處汗如漿
絡繹難延六月涼
若羨郎君登第早
須將柳葉換薯莨

——陳坤

261

* 薯莨，俗稱狗尾草，其根為染料。
* Shu-liang: Pennisetum japonecum, a creeping
plant whose roots are good for dyeing.

收買狗　　　　　　　　　　Buying Dog

268

竹枝詞

日方長至一陰生
濁氣乘時律不清
狡兔何曾三窟盡
紛紛屠狗作新烹

——陳坤

A Physiognomist 看相先生

竹枝詞

大書相法獨稱神
惹得游人靜聽頻
自命直談無忌諱
果然氣色驗來真

——頤安主人

Selling Flower 賣花

竹枝詞

魚藻門前縐綠波
渡頭斜對艷情繁
憐香蝴蝶成團見
低逐賣花人過河

——陳春榮

十九世紀中國市井風情

竹枝詞

给牌挂號赴官圍
獵犬奔馳兔欲飛
攜得山禽兼野獸
知從野外打槍歸

——王昌南

打獵　　　　　　　　　　　　Hunting

271

賣皮墊　　　　　　Selling Leather Cushion

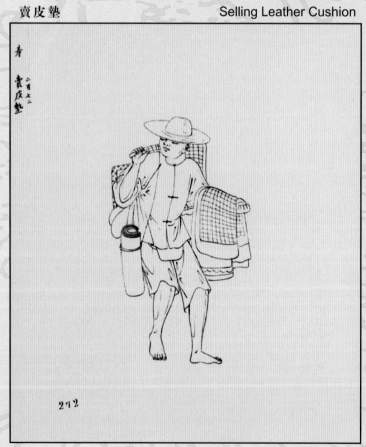

272

三百六十行 360 PROFESSION

十九世紀中國市井風情

Making Su-bao　　　　　　　　　做蘇包

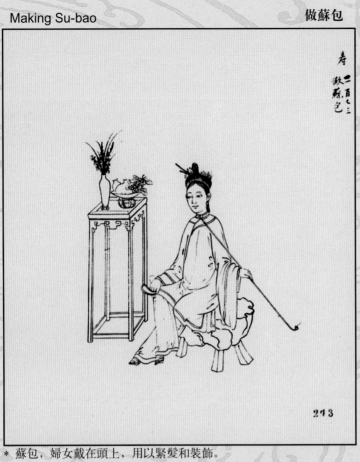

273

* 蘇包，婦女戴在頭上，用以緊髮和裝飾。
* Su-bao: Woman's head band, is used for pressing hair and adorning.

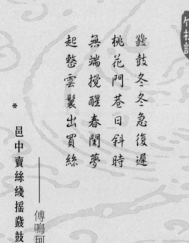

竹枝詞

鼗鼓冬冬急復遲
桃花門巷日斜時
無端攪醒春閨夢
起整雲鬟出買絲

* 邑中賣絲綫搖鼗鼓。

——傅鳴珂

Reeling Silk　　　　　　　　　絞絲

274

十九世紀中國市井風情

捶金箔　　　　　　　　　　Hammering Gold Foil

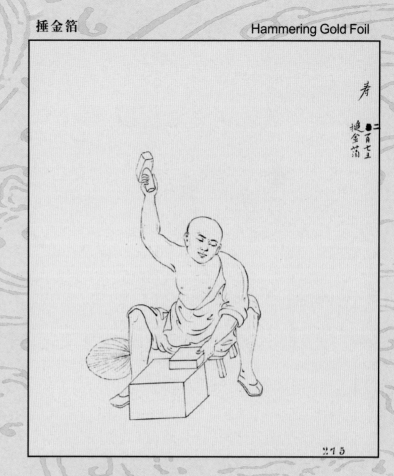

趕豬郎　　　　　　　　　A Man Driving Pig

三百六十行 360 PROFESSION

十九世紀中國市井風情

A Performance with Drum　　演鼓花

壽

演鼓花

二百七七

深哇小唱數營前
妝點風流美少年
長日演來三腳戲
采茶歌到試茶天

——陳文瑞

Selling Fish Lantern　　賣魚燈

二百六
賣魚燈

竹枝詞

花燈萬點月初升
彩結燈棚夜色凝
爆竹聲傳春意鬧
家家兒子鬧魚燈

——鄒凌霄館

十九世紀中國市井風情

244

擔山水　Carrying Spring Water

寺
二百之九
擔山水

279

竹枝詞

至清莫若在山泉
掬取家家仔細煎
可惜濟時才小試
一肩才博幾青錢

——陳坤

做纓帽　Making Tassel Hat

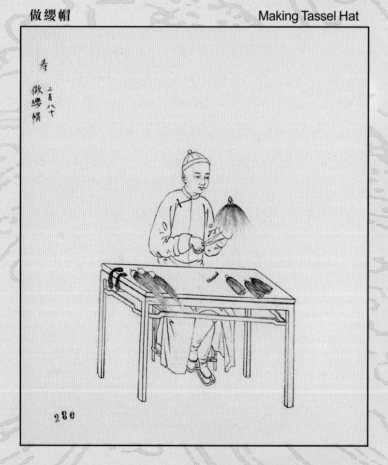

寺
二百八十
做纓帽

280

竹枝詞

老店馳名劉鶴家
三錢買得好烏紗
昨來誤怪稱呼別
乞丐相逢總稱爺

——杜濬

三百六十行 360 PROFESSIONS

Fishing　　　　　　　　　　　　　　釣魚

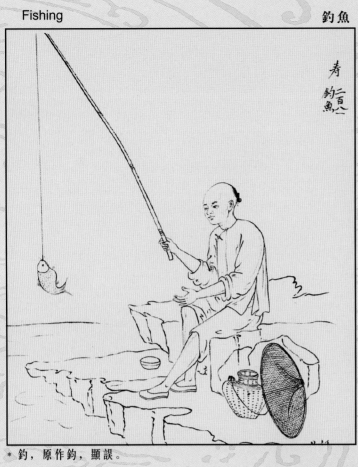

菱角雞頭爛不收
得魚換酒終朝醉
垂竿獨釣一湖秋
綠草蓑衣舴艋舟

——張實居

壽
二百
釣八
魚十

*釣，原作鈎，顯誤。

Making Stockings　　　　　　　　　　做襪

竹枝詞

絲襪通行國貨多
年來一事尤堪慰
女工歲月詎蹉跎
土布人家有織梭

——胡子晉

壽
做
百襪
八
三

十九世紀中國市井風情

246

做緯帽　　　　　　　　Making Embroidering Hat

竹枝詞

雨纓鐵杆不招風
緯帽都興一口鐘
三直緞靴須帶銃
簇新袍樣小團龍

——楊米人

賣老鼠藥　　　　　Selling Ratsbane

竹枝詞

樹邊小石祈年社
擊鼓吹螺賽伯公
薰鼠若能供薦福
伯公當保一年豐

——趙希璜

*原缺藥字，逕補。

三百六十行 360 PROFESSION

十九世紀中國市井風情

Selling Pineapple Chicken

賣波羅雞

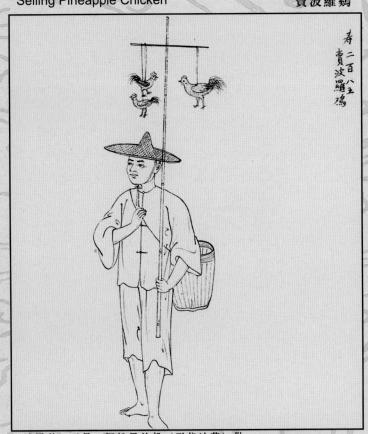

壽
二百八五
賣波羅鷄

竹枝詞

春深南海壽筵開
謁廟焚香買棹回
攜得波羅雞五色
曾瞻日出海東來

——陳坤

247

* 波羅鷄，玩具，用松果外殼（形似波蘿）做
成鷄形。
* Pineapple Chicken: a toy made of
pineapple.

Selling Sugarcane

賣蔗

竹枝詞

疏燒謝灶廿三天
白蔗條長金橘圓
爆竹聲聲除夕近
麻糖油角慶團年

——何紹塘

壽
賣蔗
二百八六

236

十九世紀中國市井風情

痴雀　　　　　　　　　　　　　　Catching Sparrow

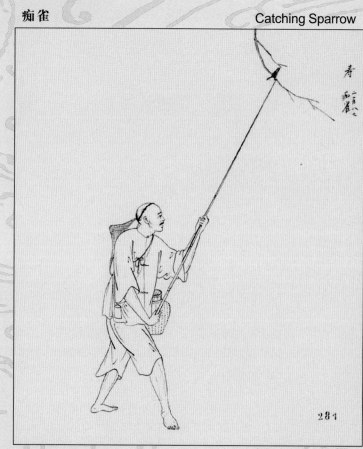

竹枝詞

秋水尋常沒釣磯
秋林隨意敞柴扉
八月田中黃雀嗚
九月盤中黃雀肥

——朱彝尊

* 痴，在粵語中有粘的意思。

賣香櫞　　　　　　　　Selling Fingered Citron

竹枝詞

第一香櫞第二蓮
第三檳榔個個圓
第四夫容五棗子
送郎都要得郎憐

——黃遵憲

* 櫞，原誤作椽。

三百六十行 360 PROFESSION

Dressing Woman　　　　催粧婆

壽
二百八九
催粧婆

289

紫花衣服著來多
打扮丫環付賣婆
急向街頭呼太太
快回鍋上烙餑餑

——杜濬

Collecting and Making Wooden Material　　　　收整木料

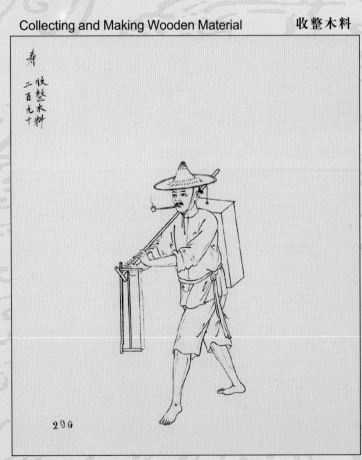

壽
收整木料
二百九十

290

竹枝詞

瀕海商場集廣陳
俞塘橋畔鮮行人
自從規復徒杠後
座市改觀百態新

——柯志頤　柯培鼎

十九世紀中國市井風情

托錢　Carrying Stringed Coins

竹枝詞

端陽臘月與中秋
店賬每逢三節收
六底銅錢九五扣
銀洋上府有抬頭

——童謙孟

壽
二百九一
托錢

291

鑣老鼠　Catching Rat

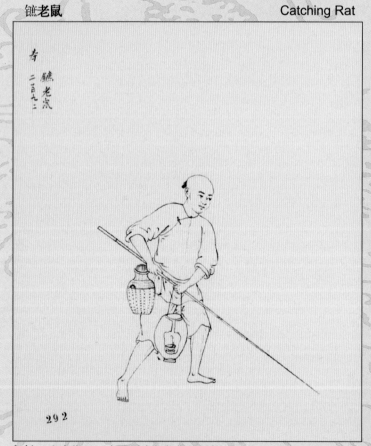

壽
二百九二
鑣老鼠

292

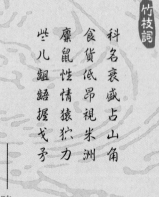

竹枝詞

科名衰盛占山角
食貨低昂視米洲
麋鼠性情猿視狃力
些儿齟齬握戈矛

——陳文瑞

* 鑣，實當作鑣，意爲用尖銳物投擲目標。

三百六十行 360 PROFESSION

Angling Frog 釣哈㟲

壽
三百九三
釣蛤蟆

293

* 哈㟲，即蛤蟆。

Making Silk Rope 打絲繩

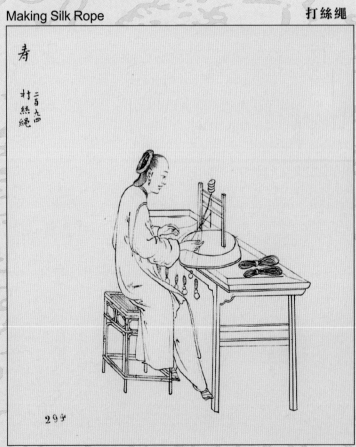

壽
三百九四
打絲繩

294

竹枝詞

蕉葉青青蕉子黃
曉妝茉莉鬢邊香
雙趺如雪通街走
黑辮紅繩未嫁娘

——彭玉麟

織網　　　　　　　　　　　Weaving Net

竹枝詞

好個鰈鰈比目魚
也隨市擔趁豪奢
勸郎且歇撈罾業
命薄如儂怕似渠

——譚石甫

賣席　　　　　　　　　　　Selling Mat

竹枝詞

五步荷花十步蘆
家家織席利錙銖
堪憐村婦多工藝
一事無成愧丈夫

——張弘弢

十九世紀中國市井風情

Building Awning　　　　　　搭棚

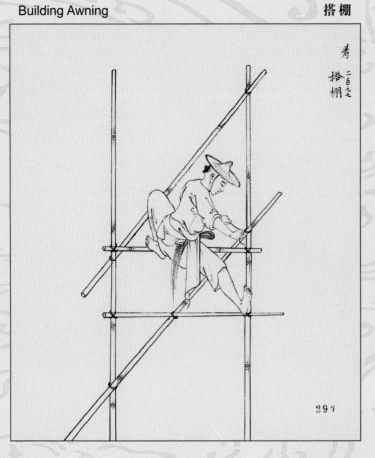

竹枝詞

東門外搭彩棚多
慶祝天妃聖誕過
賽報廟園蘭會盛
花香風里聽笙歌

——秦榮光

Selling Arrowhead　　　　　　賣茨菇

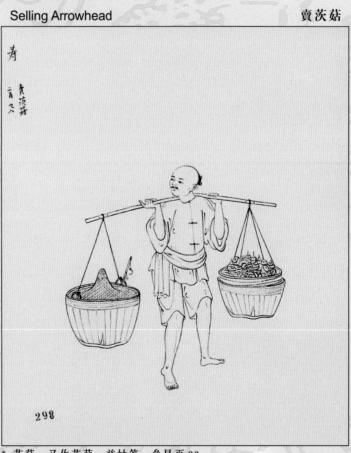

* 茨菇，又作茨菰、慈姑等。參見頁36。

十九世紀中國市井風情

賣藕　　　　　　　　　　　　Selling Lotus-root

竹枝詞

阿儂生小住河南
水國生涯未易談
白藕鮮時菱角賤
十錢買得一筠籃

——馮樹槐

剗牛皮　　　　　　　　　　Scraping Cow Hide

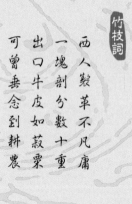

竹枝詞

西人鞣革不凡庸
一塊剖分數十重
出口牛皮如菽粟
可曾垂念到耕農

——羅四峰

* 剗，粤语俗字，意为刮削。

三百六十行 360 PROFESSION

十九世紀中國市井風情

Selling Miscellaneous Articles　　　　賣雜貨

Grinding Hot Pepper Powder　　　　研辣椒粉

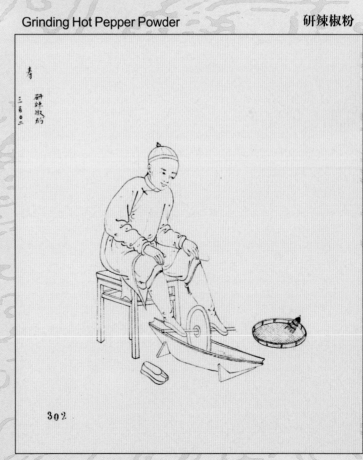

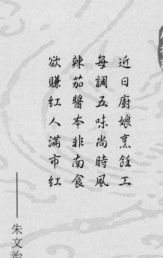

竹枝詞

近日廚娘烹飪工
每調五味尚時風
辣茄醬本非南食
欲賺紅人滿市紅

——朱文治

三百六十行 360 PROFESSIONS

十九世紀中國市井風情

256

賣橙　　　　　　　　　　　　　Selling Orange

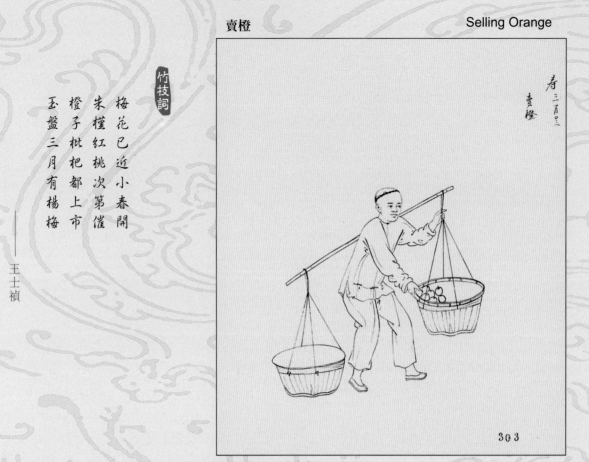

竹枝詞

梅花已近小春開
朱槿紅桃次第催
橙子枇杷都上市
玉盤三月有楊梅

——王士禎

賣算盤　　　　　　　Selling Abacus

竹枝詞

算盤眼色不須精
拉得豪商便出名
高底壞鞋尖頂帽
如今刮氣是官人

——葉調元

三百六十行 360 PROFESSIONS

十九世紀中國市井風情

Chopping Fire Wood 劈柴

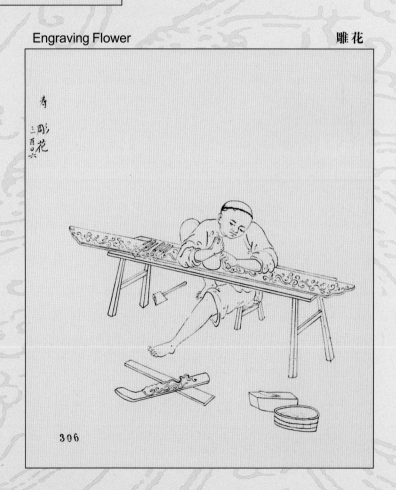

壽
三百〇五
劈柴

砍柴莫砍馬胡梢
自從戌戌荒年後
餓死甘心莫捧瓢
凍心甘心莫偷盜

——彭淑

305

* 劈，原作霹，顯誤。

Engraving Flower 雕花

壽
彫花
三百〇六

竹枝詞

雕刻香螺作酒杯
春愁似海知難遣
壽山花盒待郎開
玳瑁頭梳傍玉臺

——杭世駿

306

十九世紀中國市井風情

做木佬　　　　　　　　　　　　　　　　　A Carpenter

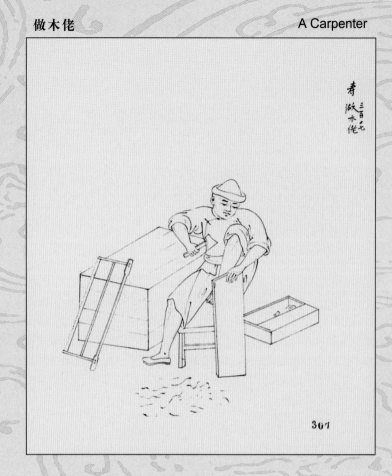

竹枝詞

登登築削幾番忙
嫁女先來定嫁裝
桶物滿房緣五鈸
銅筍打出菜花香

——童謙孟

擺果攤　　　　　　　　　　　Setting Fruit Stand

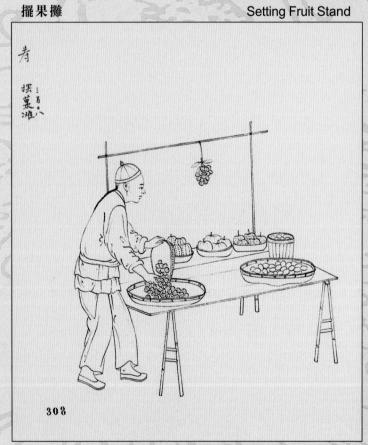

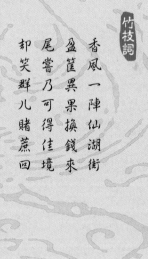

竹枝詞

香風一陣仙湖街
盈筐異果換錢來
尾嘗乃可得佳境
卻笑群兒賭蔗回

——李調元

三百六十行 360 PROFESSION

十九世紀中國市井風情

Making Rope-ring of Scale　　　　　　　　打秤耳繩

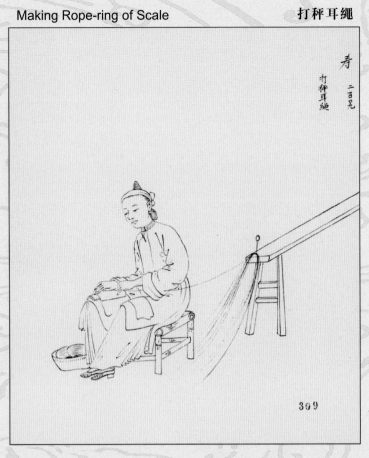

寿
竹秤耳繩
二百兄

309

Curing Teeth　　　　　　醫牙

寿
醫牙
三百十

風精提牙蚤
陽

牙科

310

竹枝詞

腹未果時汗已流
手巾頻頻拭兩鬢
津津有味且休誇
牙齒須防得劇病

——

張元垻

十九世紀中國市井風情

260

賣粉湯　　　　　　　　　　　Selling Rice-noodle Soup

竹枝詞

高朋勝友滿茶坊
有事邀來話短長
每到三更留半閘
打冬門外賣清湯

———翟金生

織籮　　　　　　　　　　　Weaving Basket

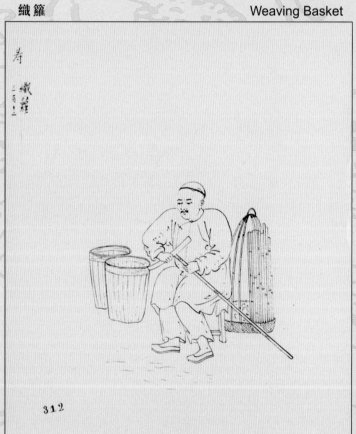

竹枝詞

芬芳滿擔露盈筐
手捧銀雲作斗量
日曬紅窗人未起
賣花人到侶新妝

———胡鶴

三百六十行 360 PROFESSIONS

十九世紀中國市井風情

Washing Silk Thread　　　　　　　洗絲綫

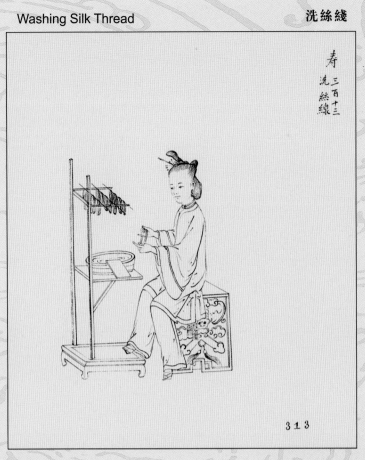

竹枝詞

織雲坊在獨兜家
翻得入時花樣巧
小婦沿溪出浣紗
銀光雪色蔴絲誇

——朱麟應

Cutting out Clothe　　　　　　　裁衣

竹枝詞

銀紅湖綢色時新
順德綢粗程蔴俗
囑母裁衣要認真
小姑預備看迎春

——陳其藻

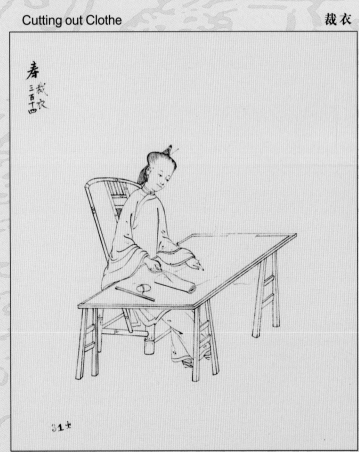

十九世紀中國市井風情

賣串炮　　　　　　　　　Selling Series Fire Cracker

竹枝詞

刺桐開遍越王臺
雞黍衫榆社又開
霹靂數聲花爆響
萬家爭賽福神來

——倪雲癯

賣繩鞋　　　　　　　　Selling Rope Sandal

竹枝詞

江城煙柳趁新晴
結伴嬉春著屐行
何用遊山雙不借
棕鞋也似筍鞋輕

——方鼎銳

三百六十行 360 PROFESSION

十九世紀中國市井風情

Weaving Bamboo Hat 　　　　　　　　織竹笠

寿
織竹笠

* 標題似有誤，實際上畫面所展示的是
　織竹籃。
* It seems some thing wrong. The picture
　shows that a man weaves bamboo basket.

317

Carving Word Block 　　　　　　　　雕字板

竹枝詞

羅家崇道有通書
合璧聯珠算不虛
試問明年河洛圖
南華街畔刻工居

——高小雲

寿
彫字板

318

十九世紀中國市井風情

264

裁縫　　　　　　　　　　　　　　　　　A Tailor

319

* 參見頁33。

油漆　　　　　　　　　　Painting

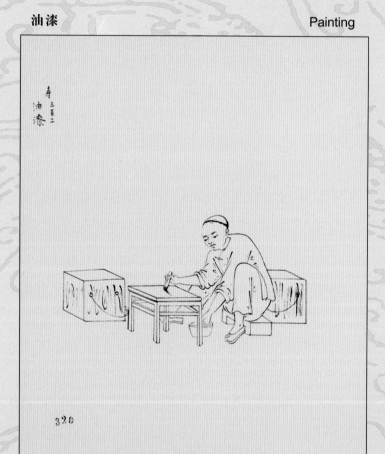

320

竹枝詞

富人棺槨講繁華
花板中心選菊花
其次對墻見許厚
一年一度漆來加

——葉調元

三百六十行 360 PROFESSION

十九世紀中國市井風情

Carrying Brick and Tile

擔磚瓦

壽
二百廿一
担磚瓦

竹枝詞

眼前突兀眼前空
木石遷移十穩中
可念舊時梁上燕
多情曾戀主人翁

——陳文瑞

321

Appeasing Ghost

設鬼

壽
設鬼
三百廿二

竹枝詞

紅燈閃閃角頻吹
夜跳茅山禳代醫
不藥本爲中治法
病魔幾見闆靈祇

——陳坤

322

十九世紀中國市井風情

266

做神像　　　　　　　Making Statue of god

竹枝詞

雪花六出最宜禾
瓶甖收藏隔歲多
鑟處塑成彌勒佛
也開眉眼笑呵呵

——朱文治

323

搬點心　　　　　　　Carrying Dian-xin

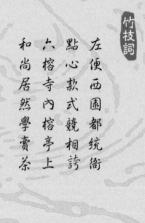

竹枝詞

左便西園都統衙
點心款式競相誇
六榕寺內榕亭上
和尚居然學賣茶

——胡子晋

324

* Dian-xin: so many kinds of small food not for regular
　meal in China.

三百六十行 360 PROFESSION

Selling Almanac　　　　　　賣通書

竹枝詞

縷析絛分算不訛
焚香元旦注如何
南華街有通書刊
推步精明讓姓羅

——陳詞翰

Digging Sweet Potato　　　　挖番薯

竹枝詞

桃源仙子飯胡麻
猶餌甘薯老歲華
此是長生真妙藥
何須更事覓丹沙

——陳坤

* 挖，原作執；薯，原作署，據標題文義改。

推碾　　　　　　　　　　　　　　　　Grinding

三言世

327

* 標題原缺，今據畫面補。
* No title on original picture,it is
added in accordance with the painting's
appearance.

賣鴨　　　　　　　Selling Duck

壽
三言廿八
賣鴨

329

竹枝詞

鴨兒有埠鴨兒肥
禾際蓬葜漸漸稀
不似仙才誇葉令
只教鳧影作雙飛

陳坤

十九世紀中國市井風情

268

十九世紀中國市井風情

Making Precision Scale　　　　　　做秤戲

壽三百廿九
做秤戲

320

Selling Reed　　　　　　賣筘

壽三百卅
賣筘

330

* 筘，又作篓，織機的一個部件。

* Reed: a spare parts of loom.

十九世紀中國市井風情

和尚募化　　　　　　　A Buddhist Monk Asking for Alms

賣棕繩　　　　　　Selling Palm Fiber Rope

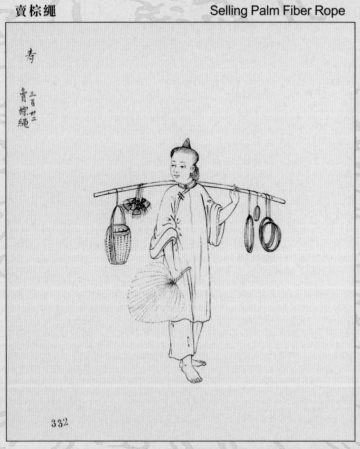

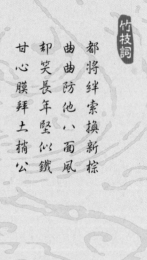

竹枝詞

都將絆索換新棕
曲曲防他八面風
卻笑長年堅似鐵
甘心膜拜土偶公

　　——周亮工

三百六十行 360 PROFESSION

Grinding Rice Grain 　　　　磨穀

＊磨，原作砳，俗字。

Carrying Grain 　　　　擔穀

竹枝詞

村村秋稼望如雲
總銖平收主佃分
更有納租升斗計
和將秕穮送東君

——陳文瑞

十九世紀中國市井風情

272

打鐵　　　　　　　　　　　　　　　　A Blacksmith

335

竹枝詞

國初刀造濮元良
家住南城善鑄鋼
近日用場鋼倍大
輪機製造仿西洋

——秦榮光

寫燈籠　　　　　　　　Writing on Lantern

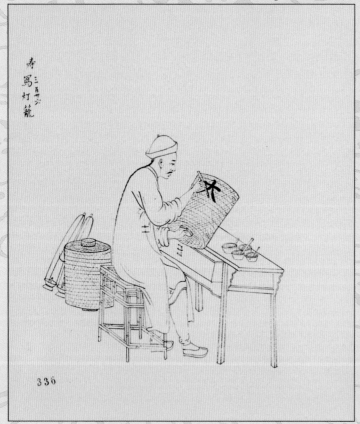

336

竹枝詞

飛到肩興總似風
闐人穿過路當中
浪題花字憑君認
斗大燈籠一朵紅

——李汝謙

三百六十行 360 PROFESSION

Selling Red Charm　賣紅錢

竹枝詞

一路花紅撒紙錢
嫁娘啼過似堪憐
鬢梢袖底釵相換
未入郎家早結緣

——陳文瑞

337

Selling Steamed Sugar Cane　賣熟蔗

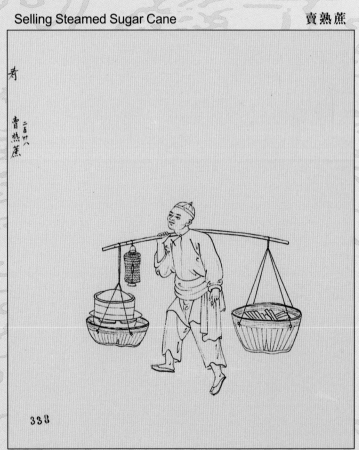

338

十九世紀中國市井風情

賣梳篦   Selling Comb

旗下仔   A Manchurian

三百六十行 360 PROFESSION

Inserting Seedlings　　　　　　　　　　　　　插秧

寿
二百卅一
插央

竹枝詞

栽秧插禾滿村啼
正是栽秧插禾時
口唱秧歌騎快馬
晚來還帶詐包歸

——彭淑

3卅1

* 秧，原作央，顯訛。

Hoeing Weeds　　　　　　　　　　　　　耘草

竹枝詞

鳴鳩聲裏蒔禾忙
容易秋風稻又黃
蘆管競吹田子了
兒童歡喜慶豐穰

——陳坤

寿
芸草
二百四十二

3卅2

* 耘，原作芸，音近而訛。

竹枝詞

火藥局邊紅莧遲
恰同上市白鱗鰣
滿肩多是江鄉味
臥聽街頭賣荸薺

——翟金生

水鷄賣馬蹄 A Boat Girl Selling Water Chestnut

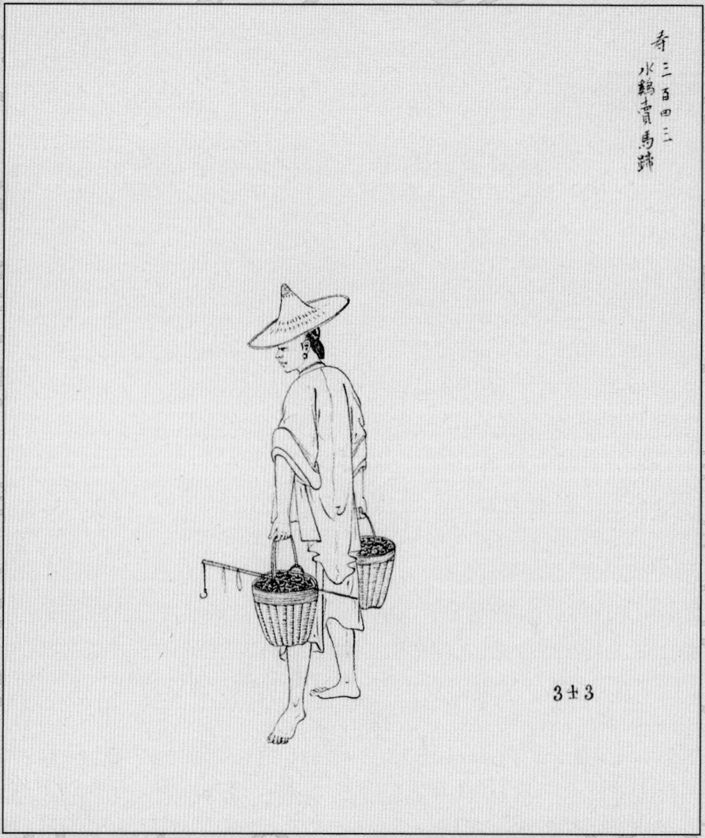

* 水鷄，當時對疍家女子的蔑稱。

賣毛掃 Selling Feather Broom

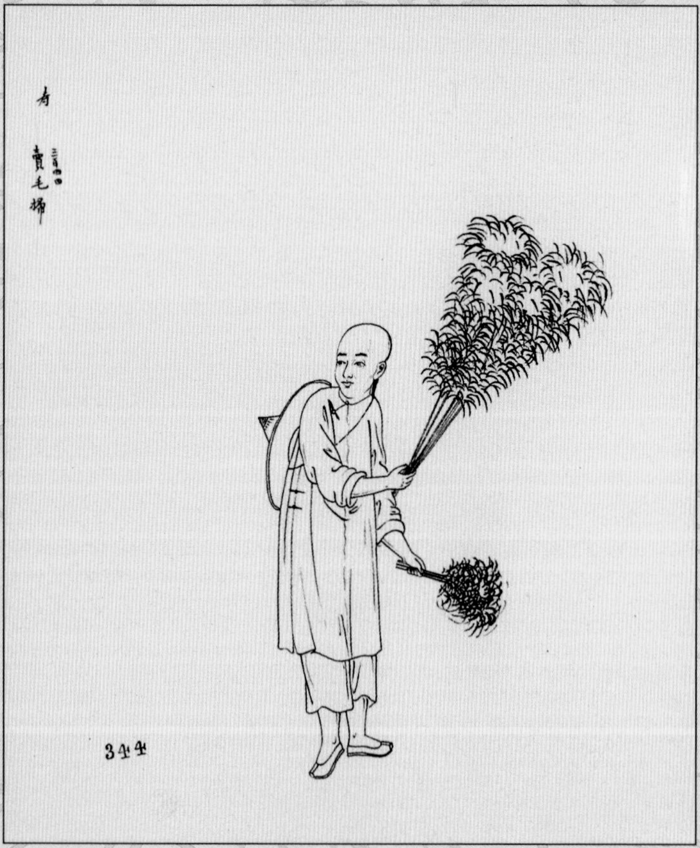

* 參見頁5。

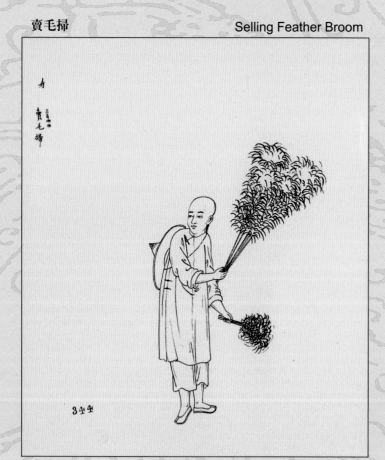

十九世紀中國市井風情

Grinding Herb Powder 研藥末

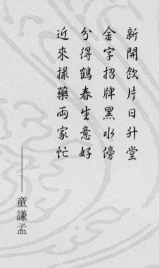

竹枝詞

新開飲片日升堂
金字招牌黑水傍
分得鶴春生意好
近來攝藥兩家忙

——童謙孟

277

Insane Girl 發瘋妹

竹枝詞

能醫麻毒太奇新
廣告街招着手春
易氏沃林傳妙藥
却敎依舊有瘋人

——胡子晉

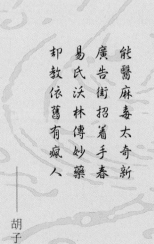

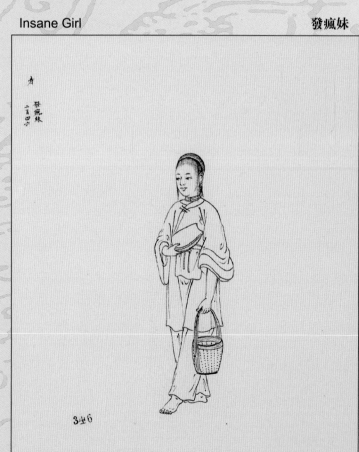

十九世紀中國市井風情

278

磨鑑　　　　　　　　　　　　　Grinding Mirror

3+1

＊鑑，原作鋻，俗字。

賣皮草　　　　　　　　　　　　Selling Fur

348

＊標題原缺，今據畫面補。
＊No title on original picture, it is added in accordance
with the painting's appearance.

三百六十行 360 PROFESSION

十九世紀中國市井風情

Grinding Powder Color

研顏色

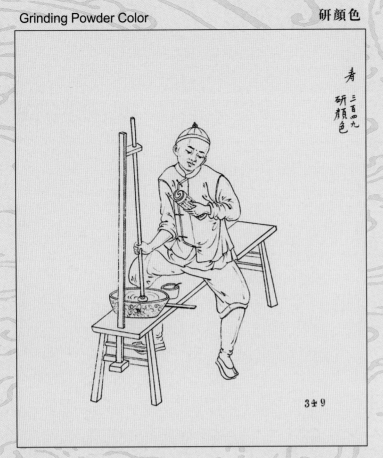

青
三百四九
研顏色

349

竹枝詞

月白似藍藍似青
染坊顏色比前深
半青被面全青樣
安得姑娘出嫁心

——童謙孟

Selling Beef

賣牛肉

竹枝詞

花布街連廣益橋
教門生意獨殷饒
糖糕切片經油脆
牛肉懸門扑鼻臊

——葉調元

青
賣牛肉
三百五十

350

十九世紀中國市井風情

280

紡麻綫　　　　　　　　　　　Spinning Hemp Thread

竹枝詞

朝采桑枝夜績麻
纖纖十指是葱芽
紫騮少年停鞭問
白苧村西第一家

——馬壽谷

繡鞋　　　　　　　　Embroidering Shoe

竹枝詞

海棠金菊步官街
步步生花士女偕
便抵貧家糧數月
繡成公子一雙鞋

——梁信芳

Weaving Net 織網

三百五三

竹枝詞

男子向海摘魚蝦
女兒補網各看家
到門遇有投魚客
瓢舀鹽湯當吃茶

——郭麟

353

* 標題原缺，今據畫面補。

* No title on original picture, it is added
  in accordance with the painting's appearance.

Giving Moxibustion Treatment 灸麻

壽
灸
麻
三百五四

354

十九世紀中國市井風情

整針　　　　　　　　　　　　　Making Needle

竹枝詞

二排樓畔倦停針
再罷琵琶弄月琴
欲借琴弦彈妾恨
還將月鏡照郎心

——匡乃闔

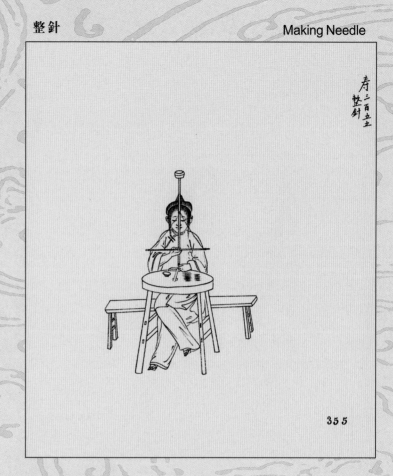

355

印字板　　　　Printing Word Plate

竹枝詞

長柄葫蘆鶴頸同
古傳此種出江東
我家套板翻新式
篆隸書精花鳥工

——秦榮光

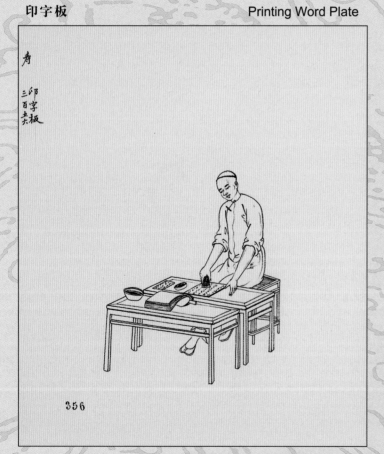

356

三百六十行 360 PROFESSION

Selling Eggs of Chicken and Duck 賣鷄鴨蛋

壽
賣鷄鴨蛋
三百五七

357

Singing Divined Information 唱卦知

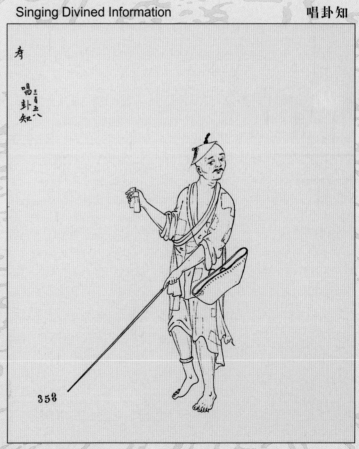

壽
唱卦知
三百五八

358

十九世紀中國市井風情

賣茶果　　　　　　　　　　　　Selling Tea Snack

竹枝詞

采茶忙是一春忙
焙茶芽屋生幽香
茶子不教人摘取
苦心留與世間嘗

——趙希璜

賣京包　　　　　　　　　　Selling Beijing Purse

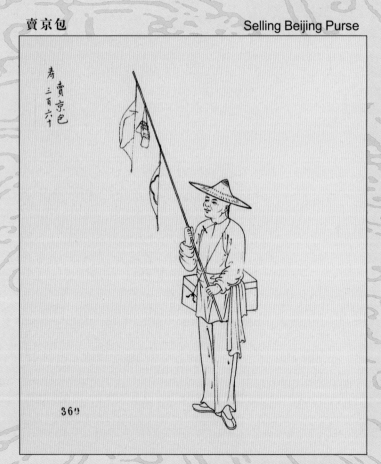